Vergil's
Aeneid
8 & 11

Vergil's *Aeneid*

8 & 11: Italy & Rome

Barbara Weiden Boyd

Bolchazy-Carducci Publishers, Inc.
Wauconda, Illinois USA

General Editor
Laurie Haight Keenan

Cover Design & Typography
Adam Phillip Velez

Cover Image
Sandro Botticelli, *Pallas/Camilla and the Centaur* (detail). Tempera on wood.
Erich Lessing / Art Resource, NY

Vergil's Aeneid 8 & 11
Italy & Rome

Barbara Weiden Boyd

The Latin text of *Aeneid* 8.608–731, 11.498–596, and 11.664–835
is from *P. Vergili Maronis Opera* (Oxford, 1969; repr. with corrections, 1972)
R. A. B Mynors, ed., by permission of Oxford University Press.

Bolchazy-Carducci Publishers, Inc.
1000 Brown Street
Wauconda, IL 60084 USA
www.bolchazy.com

Printed in the United States of America
2006
by United Graphics

ISBN-13: 978-0-86516-580-9
ISBN-10: 0-86516-580-7

Library of Congress Cataloging-in-Publication Data

Virgil.
  [Aeneis. Selections.]
  Vergil's Aeneid 8 & 11: Italy & Rome / Barbara Weiden Boyd.
    p. cm.
  Latin and English.
  Includes bibliographical references.
  ISBN-13: 978-0-86516-580-9 (pbk.)
  ISBN-10: 0-86516-580-7 (pbk.)
  1. Aeneas (Legendary character)--Poetry. 2. Latin language--Readers--Poetry. 3.
Epic poetry, Latin. I. Boyd, Barbara Weiden, 1952- II. Title.

PA6801.A45 2001
873'.01--dc22

2006009564

Contents

Introduction

This edition of selections from Books 8 and 11 of Vergil's *Aeneid* is the first in a series of supplements to my textbook, *Vergil's Aeneid: Selections from Books 1, 2, 4, 6, 10, and 12* (second edition, 2004). The widespread popularity of Clyde Pharr's school edition of the first six books of the *Aeneid* (*Vergil's Aeneid Books 1–6* [Lexington, MA: D.C. Heath, 1930; repr. 1964]; now repr. by Bolchazy-Carducci) in Latin courses at both the high school and undergraduate levels has made it seem sensible to me to continue to emulate at least formally the layout and particular virtues of Pharr's edition. I shall indicate more precisely under the separate headings below those features of Pharr's textbook I have adapted for use here, as well as those places where I diverge. Teachers and students familiar with my earlier *Aeneid* textbooks from Bolchazy-Carducci will find here a continuation of the approach I initiated in those books, although I have allowed myself to be a bit more expansive in some of my background comments here than was previously the case; given the relative density of historical and mythical detail in these selections, fuller notes seemed not only appropriate but necessary.

As I noted in my introduction to *Vergil's Aeneid 10 & 12: Pallas & Turnus* (1998), it has become increasingly difficult to find appropriate, available, and affordable editions of the second half of the *Aeneid*, in whole or in part. At the same time, the decision made by the Advanced Placement Latin Test Development Committee (working on behalf of the Educational Testing Service) in 1999 to add selections from the second half of the *Aeneid* to the AP Latin syllabus has drawn new attention to the half of the poem neglected by Pharr. I am delighted to have this opportunity, therefore, to introduce readers to several episodes that can only enrich and deepen their appreciation for and understanding of Vergil's poetic project. The selections chosen for presentation here will, I hope, serve the particular interests of those concerned with Vergil's representation of both myth and history, both past and future, in the *Aeneid*: on the one hand, the triumphant celebration of Octavian's defeat of his enemies at Actium on the divine shield given to the uncomprehending Aeneas, and on the other the defeat, through trickery and misplaced desire, of the heroic Camilla—called "Italy's ornament" by her ally Turnus—are juxtaposed here in order to invite scrutiny of the relationship, both strained and intimate, between Italy and Rome, and of Vergil's complex understanding of that relationship.

I close with heartfelt thanks to all those who have helped me assemble this text: Laurie Haight Keenan, who has once again ensured the adherence of this text to Bolchazy-Carducci's standards, and has shown me unwonted patience in the process; Margaret Brucia, whose continuing support of my textbook work on the *Aeneid* has expressed itself in countless rewarding conversations of Vergil's poetry; and Katherine Bradley, who not only assembled the vocabulary lists for this book but who also read through and commented on every word in these notes. That Katherine did so even through a period of personal challenge is abundant testimony not only to her dedication to teaching and her rigorous high standards, but also to her devotion to all matters Vergilian. I have been honored to work with her and to know her friendship. Any errors of fact or judgment that remain are of course my own.

BARBARA WEIDEN BOYD
Bowdoin College

Features of the Text and Notes

Text

The text used here is that printed in R. A. B. Mynors' 1969 edition (reprinted with corrections, 1972) of the Oxford Classical Text of Vergil. I have made a few cosmetic alterations to make this text more congenial to the intermediate Latin student: the initial letters of words beginning a new sentence are printed in the upper case; and third-declension accusative plural nouns and adjectives ending in **-is** are here printed as ending in **-es.** Both of these alterations are in keeping with Pharr's treatment of the text.

Orthography

In keeping with contemporary usage (as well as the format followed by Pharr), I have printed consonantal **u** as **v.** Consonantal **i,** however, remains **i** throughout the text and notes. Thus, the Latin names of the king and queen of the gods appear as **Iuppiter** and **Iuno.**

Subdivisions of the Text

For convenience's sake, I have subdivided all of the selections in this textbook into smaller subsections, and have introduced each with a brief descriptive heading. These subdivisions are not meant to be canonical, and students should be alerted to the fact that these subdivisions are a modern addition to Vergil's text. I have simply attempted to suggest to teachers and students logical places in the text for a pause and perhaps for discussion.

Vocabulary Lists

A running vocabulary list appears on each page of Latin text, and an alphabetical list of all vocabulary glossed appears at the end of the text. In determining what vocabulary is to be glossed, I have used Pharr's general Word List as a guide and have not glossed the words on this list. In addition, I have incorporated into my expectation of students' working vocabulary those words that Pharr includes in his list of words found 12–23 times in *Aeneid* 1–6. Thus, teachers can raise their expectations of their students' working vocabulary as they turn to the selections in this book, and add the words on this list to their regular vocabulary drills. Given the brevity of the selections included in this text, I have glossed new proper names and epithets only once, i.e., the first time they appear.

Macrons

The Latin text, running vocabulary, and lemmata in the notes appear without macrons. Students should be encouraged to realize that the Romans did not write with macrons (nor do ancient manuscripts generally feature word division, punctuation, or a distinction between upper- and lower-case letters!). They should also be encouraged to practice scansion on a text without macrons. I have, however, included macrons in the alphabetical vocabulary at the end of the book. This provides to teachers and students alike a source for quick consultation.

Rhetorical Terms and Figures of Speech

I have included immediately before the vocabulary a glossary of the rhetorical terms and figures of speech used in this supplement. In most cases, I have simply adapted Pharr's original definitions to examples chosen from the selections in this textbook.

Abbreviations

I have kept abbreviations in the vocabulary and notes to a minimum, and have tempted to avoid any source of confusion. Thus, "nom.," "gen.," "dat.," "acc.," and "abl.," as well as other familiar abbreviations, are used here; but wherever confusion might result, e.g., between "subj." ("subject") and "subj." ("subjunctive"), I have not abbreviated the terminology used.

In the vocabulary lists, I have abbreviated only the second principal part of verbs (first conjugation verbs are indicated by a (1) in place of a full listing of principal parts). The genitive forms of third-declension nouns, when abbreviated, are intended to show students the root of a given word.

Grammatical and Syntactical Terminology

In the teaching of Latin in the schools, a wide variety of terminology for grammatical and syntactical constructions is current. Thus, for example, the subject-accusative + infinitive construction with verbs of knowing, saying, thinking, etc., is more commonly learned in American schools as "indirect discourse" or "indirect statement" (and also, albeit much less frequently, as "oratio obliqua"). In choosing to call this construction "indirect statement" in the notes, I am not endorsing a particular method or otherwise attempting to offer a value judgment on the available terminology; rather, I am attempting to represent to the best of my ability, based on over twenty-five years of college teaching and nine years with the Advanced Placement Latin Test Development Committee, the terminology most likely to be familiar to students reading at this level.

The real test of a commentary of this sort is the degree to which it allows students to read Latin independently; I hope that my commentary can make this possible in as unobtrusive a manner as possible.

Teachers and students should also note that I frequently offer two possible interpretations for a given construction (e.g., on 11.704, I comment on the lemma **consilio ... et astu**, "abl. of means or of description"). My purpose in offering these alternatives is not to cause confusion, but to suggest to students that their instincts are often right when they are puzzled by the ambiguity of a particular construction. This occasion also offers teachers an opportunity to remind their students that terms such as "abl. of cause" and "dat. of agent" are artificial constructs—no Roman reader would have needed, or understood, these categories.

Interpretive Comments

While I have not engaged in lengthy discussions of the interpretation of a given passage or subsection, I have on occasion permitted myself to comment on features of Vergil's style that repay close examination. I have attempted to make these comments in an "open," that is, suggestive, manner, rather than as "closed" and definitive statements of Vergil's purpose. I hope that these comments will offer to teachers and students the opportunity for rewarding discussion of the complexities of Vergil's poem.

For a fuller introduction to the interpretation of the *Aeneid*, see the critical works cited in the Bibliography at the end of the commentary.

SELECTIONS FROM VERGIL'S *AENEID*
BOOK 8.608–731

The Shield of Aeneas—Introduction

The outbreak of war soon follows the arrival of Aeneas and the Trojans in Italy; the Latin followers of king Latinus, led by the Rutulian Turnus, assemble and plan their defense (Book 7). Meanwhile, Aeneas lands on the shore at a bend in the river Tiber, where a group of Arcadians from the Greek mainland has settled. The place is called Pallanteum; it is ruled by the Arcadian king Evander, whose son Pallas greets the newcomers and escorts them to his father. After welcoming the Trojans, Evander proceeds to preside at a religious ceremony in honor of Hercules, an earlier visitor who had saved Evander and his people from a cattle-stealing monster; Evander explains the story behind the ritual, and invites the Trojan leader to share in his hospitality. To demonstrate the alliance thus forged between the two peoples, Evander entrusts Pallas to Aeneas as a comrade in arms against the imminent threat from Turnus and his followers; the stage is thus set for Aeneas, with the help of Evander and Pallas, to wage a successful campaign against the Latins.

8.608–25: Having ordered his troops to stay in their new camp and not to go into battle yet, Aeneas leaves Pallanteum, the Arcadian settlement on the Tiber that is destined to become the site of Rome. He heads up the river with a few companions; there, his mother finds him in a secluded grove, and presents him with the armor especially crafted for him by her husband Vulcan.

> At Venus aetherios inter dea candida nimbos
> dona ferens aderat; natumque in valle reducta
> ut procul egelido secretum flumine vidit,   610

---

aetherius, -a, -um ethereal, heavenly
candidus, -a, -um gleaming, dazzling whiter
reductus, -a, -um drawn back, remote, distant

secerno, -ere, secrevi, secretus separate, cut off
valles, -is, *f.* valley, vale

---

608. **At**: the particle is strongly adversative, i.e., it marks the change of focus from the preceding lines, describing activities on earth, to the new focus on Venus in the sky. **aetherios inter dea candida nimbos**: the word-order reflects the meaning of the words. Venus enters like the divinities of Greek tragedy, descending into the scene from above; like the tragic *deus ex machina* (lit., "god from a machine," i.e., a god brought on stage by means of a crane-like contraption), Venus appears when human effort can do no more.

609. **dona**: the new weapons, to be described in detail below.

609–10. **in valle reducta**: the participle, together with the words **procul** and **secretum** in the next line, emphasizes Aeneas' isolation. The setting is ideal for a divine epiphany.

talibus adfata est dictis seque obtulit ultro:
"En perfecta mei promissa coniugis arte
munera. Ne mox aut Laurentes, nate, superbos
aut acrem dubites in proelia poscere Turnum."
615   Dixit, et amplexus nati Cytherea petivit,
arma sub adversa posuit radiantia quercu.
Ille deae donis et tanto laetus honore

---

adversus, -a, -um facing, in front

amplexus, -us, *m.* embracing, caress, loving embrace

Cytherea, -ae, *f.* Venus, goddess of Cythera, a Greek island close to which Venus was born from the foam of the sea

dubito (1) be in doubt, hesitate

en behold! look!

Laurentes, -um, *m. pl.* the Laurentines, inhabitants of Laurentum, a sea town in Latium

mox *adv.* soon

offero, offerre, obtuli, oblatus present, offer, bring before

perficio, -ere, perfeci, perfectus complete, finish, carry out

posco, -ere, poposci demand, request; call, summon

proelium, -i, *n.* battle

promitto, -ere, promisi, promissus send forth, promise, foretell

quercus, -us, *f.* oak, oaktree

radians, -ntis beaming, shining, gleaming

Turnus, -i, *m.* Turnus, leader of the Rutulians and opponent of Aeneas

ultro *adv.* of one's own accord, voluntarily

---

611. **seque obtulit ultro**: note the rapidity and initiative with which Venus crosses the vast space between Aeneas and her—she has moved from the clouds of heaven to his presence within four swift lines.

612. **En**: the interjection suggests that Venus is pointing out the weapons as she speaks. **promissa ... arte**: The first word refers to Venus' promise to Aeneas, the second, to Vulcan's handiwork.

613. The ENJAMBMENT of **munera**, combined with its position on the page immediately below **en**, emphasizes the importance of this divine gift. **Laurentes ... superbos**: the epithet shows Venus' opposition to the enemies of her son. The Laurentes are the people ruled by king Latinus; they have joined with the Rutulians under Turnus' leadership to oppose the Trojans.

615. **amplexus nati Cytherea petivit**: Venus' behavior here is very different from that she exhibited in her encounter with Aeneas in Book 1.314–20, 402–17. There, she had eluded contact with her son; here, she seeks him out. **Cytherea**: the epithet is derived from the name of the island Cythera, one of several where Venus was said to have come ashore shortly after her birth.

615–16. **petivit ... posuit**: Venus' actions follow immediately upon one another, as she hastens to assure Aeneas of her maternal goodwill.

617. **donis et tanto ...honore**: perhaps to be understood as an instance of HENDIADYS, i.e., "at the honor of so great a gift."

expleri nequit atque oculos per singula volvit,
miraturque interque manus et bracchia versat
terribilem cristis galeam flammasque vomentem,　　　　620
fatiferumque ensem, loricam ex aere rigentem,
sanguineam, ingentem, qualis cum caerula nubes
solis inardescit radiis longeque refulget;

---

aes, aeris, *n.* bronze

bracchium, -i, *n.* arm, branch

caerul(e)us, -a, -um dark blue, dark, celestial

crista, -ae, *f.* crest of a helmet, plume

expleo, -ere, explevi, expletus fill, appease, satisfy

fatifer, -era, -erum death-dealing, deadly, destructive

galea, -ae, *f.* helmet

inardesco, -ere, inarsi burn, glow, gleam

longe *adv.* a long way off, from afar

lorica, -ae, *f.* leather cuirass

miror (1) be amazed, marvel at

nequeo, -ire, nequivi be unable, cannot

nubes, -is, *f.* cloud

qualis, -e such (as)

radius, -i, *m.* beam, ray

refulgeo, -ere, refulsi flash back, reflect, shine bright, glitter

rigeo, -ere be stiff

sanguineus, -a, -um bloody, of blood, blood-red

singuli, -ae, -a separate, individual, single

terribilis, -e dreadful, terrible, terrifying

verso (1) turn, roll, turn over

vomo, -ere, vomui, vomitus discharge, spew, pour forth, emit

---

618. **expleri:** the virtual equivalent of **se explere**, the pass. inf. here plays the role of the middle inf. in Greek. **per singula:** anticipates the long description to follow.

620. **terribilem cristis galeam flammasque vomentem:** the word for "helmet," **galeam**, appears at the center of the line, with its two epithets at either end. But is the reader really to imagine that the helmet belches forth flames? The ambiguity here anticipates the illusory vividness of the description to follow.

621. **fatiferum:** again the description anticipates what is to come—now however not in the description of the shield that completes Book 8, but in the rest of the *Aeneid*, culminating in the final lines. **ex aere:** abl. of material or of cause. **rigentem:** lit.,

"stiff from bronze": the breastplate is stiff because of, or as a result of, the material used to make it.

622. **sanguineam, ingentem:** the combination of elision with lack of connective here is striking, perhaps evoking Aeneas' stream of thought as he gazes at the handiwork of Vulcan. **sanguineam:** the epithet indicates both the color of the metal used to craft the breastplate and its effect on those who confront the hero wearing it.

622-23. **qualis …refulget:** the SIMILE for the armor's brightness seems straightforward, although the brilliance of the armor is compared not with the rays of the sun themselves, but with the clouds reflecting the rays of the sun.

tum leves ocreas electro auroque recocto,
625   hastamque et clipei non enarrabile textum. *included in test March 14. in test*

---

clipeus, -i, *m.* (*or* **clipeum, -i,** *n.*) round
  shield
electrum, -i, *n.* mixed metal (amber in
  color), electrum
enarrabilis, -e that can be described or
  explained, "describable"
hasta, -ae, *f.* spear

levis, -e smooth
ocrea, -ae, *f.* greave
recoquo, -ere, recoxi, recoctus cook again,
  reforge
textum, -i, *n.* that which is fitted together,
  structure, texture

---

624. **electro auroque recocto:** abl. of description or of material. The participle refers to the fact that the metal has been smelted repeatedly, and so purified.

625. **clipei non enarrabile textum:** the shield is mentioned last, and will remain the focus of attention for the remainder of Book 8. **non enarrabile:** is Vergil challenging his readers, or himself? By asserting the indescribability of the shield, Vergil both acknowledges that every act of viewing is partial and biased, and invites his readers to wonder at both included and excluded features in the ensuing ECPHRASIS. **textum:** the word is precisely used of something woven or layered, and so is an apt metaphor for both the shield, made of many layers of metal, and Vergil's description of it.

8.626–70: The description of the shield crafted by Vulcan for Aeneas begins. In this extended ECPHRASIS, numerous episodes from Roman history are depicted or alluded to, with abundant visual detail. It is nonetheless extremely difficult, if not impossible, to identify the precise location of each of these scenes on the shield; Vergil thus develops narrative tension, not only through the episodes he selects and juxtaposes—either in the text, or on the shield, or both—but also through the exclusion of so many other important events in Roman history. This tension also serves to emphasize the difference between the primary viewer of the shield, Aeneas, and Vergil's readers, who "see" it only through his eyes—for while Aeneas is gazing upon a history that has yet to happen, and still lies in his and Rome's future, we (and all of Vergil's readers beginning with Augustus himself) are "looking" at the past.

The description of Aeneas' shield is frequently described as a narrative PROLEPSIS (adj.: *proleptic*), "anticipation." This term is used to identify a narrative effect that introduces into a sequential narrative events that in fact happen only after the main story-line ends, and which thus interrupts the narrative sequence. The opposite device is ANALEPSIS, used by Vergil in several other ECPHRASES, including the scenes on the temple of Juno at Carthage at Book 1.456–93 and on the doors of the temple of Apollo at Book 6.20–30.

Since antiquity, readers have recognized that the ECPHRASIS of Aeneas' shield is modeled on the ECPHRASIS of Achilles' shield developed by Homer at *Iliad* 18.483–608. This similarity clearly indicates Aeneas' heroic status; at the same time, however, the many differences between the two shields suggest the importance of careful reading and reflection in comparing the two men and the two poems.

> Illic res Italas Romanorumque triumphos
> haud vatum ignarus venturique inscius aevi
> fecerat ignipotens, illic genus omne futurae

---

aevum, -i, *n.* age, life-span
ignipotens, -ntis potent in fire, ruler of fire, powerful in fire
illic *adv.* there, yonder
inscius, -a, -um not knowing, ignorant

Italus, -a, -um Italian, having to do with Italy
Romanus, -a, -um Roman, having to do with Rome
triumphus, -i, *m.* triumph, triumphal procession

---

626. **res Italas**: i.e., Roman history. The adj. **Italus** embraces the whole Italian peninsula, which by the beginning of the 3rd century BCE was entirely under Roman control. **Romanorumque triumphos**: the triumph was a great ritual procession into the city of Rome, granted by the Senate only to those generals who had won particularly noteworthy victories in battle. Its mention here in the first line of the ECPHRASIS both sets the triumphant tone of the passage as a whole and looks ahead to the final scene

on the shield, describing Octavian's triple triumph of 29 BCE.

626–28. **Illic ... , illic**: ANAPHORA, reinforced by ASYNDETON.

627. **haud vatum ignarus**: **haud** = **non** and is to be taken with both **ignarus** and **inscius**, creating a LITOTES.

628. **ignipotens**: the compound adj. is a mark of lofty epic style, going back to Homer. Here, the adj. also allows Vergil to omit Vulcan's name and to identify him instead through his divine attributes.

offspring from Ascanius

> stirpis ab Ascanio pugnataque in ordine bella.
> 630   Fecerat et viridi fetam Mavortis in antro
> procubuisse lupam, geminos huic ubera circum   *the twin boys playing around her teats hanging from her teats,*
> ludere pendentes pueros et lambere matrem   *and the mother to*
> impavidos, illam tereti cervice reflexa   *lick the fearless boys.*

and she soothes them in turn with her smooth

Ascanius, -i, *m.* Ascanius, son of Aeneas

cervix, cervicis, *f.* neck

fetus, -a, -um pregnant

impavidus, -a, -um fearless, undaunted

lambo, -ere, lambi lick

ludo, -ere, lusi, lusus play

lupa, -ae, *f.* she-wolf

Mavors, Mavortis, *m.* Mars, god of war

pendeo, -ere, pependi hang, hang from, hang around

procumbo, -ere, procubui, procubitus bend forward, lie down

pugno (1) fight, combat

reflecto, -ere, reflexi, reflectus bend back, turn back

stirps, stirpis, *f.* offspring, descendant

teres, teretis smooth

uber, uberis, *n.* teat, udder, breast

viridis, -e green

628–29. futurae stirpis ab Ascanio: the emphasis on the future in this passage is effected not only by the use of several fut. act. participles (**venturi, futurae**) but also by the identification of Ascanius, rather than Aeneas himself, as the progenitor of the Roman people.

629. in ordine: Vergil thus suggests that the scenes depicted on the shield follow an historical sequence; but where is the starting-point on a circular shield?

630. Fecerat: he had crafted, i.e., he had depicted; acc. and inf. construction, to be translated like indir. statement, follows. **viridi ... Mavortis in antro:** in Vergil's time, a cave at the foot of the Palatine hill was identified at the Lupercal, i.e., the cave where the wolf (**lupa**) nursed the twins Romulus and Remus. The reference to its color suggests the colorfulness of the scenes on the shield. The association of the cave with Mars also serves as a reminder that Romulus and Remus were the sons of Mars, who had had raped their mortal mother, Rhea

Silvia (sometimes identified with the alternative name Ilia). The name **Mavors** is an archaic version of **Mars**.

631–32. procubuisse: the first of a series of infs. in the acc. and inf. construction following **fecerat** (630): "he had shown that a she-wolf had lain down ...," etc.; **ludere** is the first word of the second infinitival phrase; note the ASYNDETON. **geminos ... pueros:** Romulus and Remus are never identified by name. **huic:** i.e., the she-wolf; dative of reference. **ubera circum:** the usual word order is inverted (ANASTROPHE).

632–33. lambere matrem impavidos: the inf. and acc. construction is the source of potential confusion here, since both the subject and the dir. obj. of the inf. are put into the acc. **lambere** introduces the third infinitival phrase; its subject is **impavidos**, describing the twins; **matrem** is the acc. dir. obj. in apposition with the implied obj. **eam**, i.e., "they licked her as if she were their mother."

neck bent back and shapes their bodies with her tongue.

mulcere alternos et corpora fingere lingua.
Nec procul hinc Romam et raptas sine more Sabinas   635
consessu caveae, magnis Circensibus actis,
addiderat, subitoque novum consurgere bellum

---

alternus, -a, -um one after the other, by turns

cavea, -ae, *f.* part of the theater where spectators sat, theater

Circenses, -ium, *m. pl.* games held in the Circus Maximus

consessus, -us, *m.* a sitting together, an assembly

consurgo, -ere, -surrexi, -surrectus rise, arise

fingo, -ere, finxi, fictus stroke, form, shape

lingua, -ae, *f.* tongue; language

mulceo, -ere, mulsi, mulsus touch lightly, caress, soothe

Roma, -ae, *f.* Rome

Sabinus, -a, -um Sabine, having to do with the Sabines, an ancient Italian people adjoining the Latins

subito *adv.* suddenly, unexpectedly

633–34. **illam … mulcere … et … fingere**: the ASYNDETON marks the shift of focus from the twins to the she-wolf, who is the subject of the fourth and fifth infinitival phrases. This shift is also emphasized by the demonstrative pronoun **illam**, with which Vergil directs his reader's visual focus away from the boys and to the she-wolf. Both infs. suggest that the very character of the boys is shaped at least in part by the she-wolf in her formative nurturing role. **alternos**: i.e., alternating between first one of the boys, then the other. **lingua**: abl. of means.

635. **Nec procul hinc**: Vergil directs us to the next series of scenes, both visually and chronologically. The verb introducing this set of scenes, however, does not appear until 637 (**addiderat**). **Romam**: note the lack of descriptive epithet; the emphasis falls entirely upon the city itself, and the fact of its existence. Aeneas thus does not see—nor are we reminded of—the events surrounding Rome's foundation, particularly the killing of Remus by Romulus. **raptas … Sabinas**: Livy 1.9–13 is our best source for this story. Shortly after building his city walls and inviting immigrants from elsewhere to settle within them, Romulus realized that a dearth of women threatened his new foundation. He therefore devised a ruse to bring

women (and children) to Rome: he invited the Sabines, a tribe living just across the Tiber river from Rome, to join the Romans for a religious festival to be held in the Circus Maximus. Caught unawares in the midst of the festivities, the Sabine women suddenly found themselves being carried off by the Roman men; the Sabine men, meanwhile, were defenseless, because they had come to the festival unarmed. **sine more**: this phrase suggests both the novelty of the event and its uncivilized character.

636. **consessu caveae**: **cavea** is used to designate the tiered seating of a theater, amphitheater, stadium, or racecourse, since in the earliest such places the seating was provided by a hollowed-out hillside. **magnis Circensibus actis**: with this abl. abs., Vergil identifies both the location (Circus Maximus) and the occasion (a prototypical version of the Ludi Magni, an annual festival held in the Circus Maximus). **actis** here has the sense "(having been) performed/ conducted," since the festival involved both numerous processions and performances.

637. **addiderat**: as with **fecerat** (630), the verb introduces another series of objects, both acc. and inf. constructions and simple accusatives. **consurgere**: inf. dependent on **addiderat**.

Romulidis Tatioque seni Curibusque severis.
Post idem inter se posito certamine, reges

640   armati Iovis ante aram paterasque tenentes
stabant et caesa iungebant foedera porca.
Haud procul inde citae Mettum in diversa quadrigae

---

armo (1) equip, furnish with weapons

caedo, -ere, cecidi, caesus cut down, kill, slaughter

citus, -a, -um quick, swift

Cures, Curium, *m. pl.* Cures, chief town of the Sabines

diversus, -a, -um turned different ways, opposite, different

foedus, foederis, *n.* treaty, league, compact

iungo, -ere, iunxi, iunctus join, unite

Mettus, -i, *m.* Mett(i)us Fufetius, an Alban general

porca, -ae, *f.* pig, sow

quadrigae, -arum, *f. pl.* team of four, four-horsed chariot

Romulidae, -arum, *m. pl.* the descendants of Romulus, the Romans

senex, senis old, aged

severus, -a, -um strict, austere, stern

Tatius, -i, *m.* Titus Tatius, a king of the Sabines

---

638. Romulidis Tatioque seni Curibusque severis: dat. of reference or advantage, indicating the three entities brought to war by the rape: the Romans, the king of the Sabines Titus Tatius, and his people, one of whose primary cities was Cures. **Romulidis**: the use of a Greek-style patronymic to identify the Romans as descendants of Romulus is both epic in style and an oblique reminder of Romulus' central role in the assault.

639. Post idem etc.: Vergil moves from indir. to dir. statement, and so from infs. to finite verbs, as he slips into historical narrative. **Post** suggests both the passage of time between the previous scene and this one, and the placement of the scene on the shield. **posito certamine**: abl. abs. **reges**: i.e., Romulus and Titus Tatius.

640. Iovis ante aram: Jupiter is an appropriate choice, since Livy tells us (1.12) that Romulus founded a temple to Jupiter Stator ('the Stayer") after his war with the Sabines. This description of Roman religious activity after war may also be meant to allude to the kingship of Numa Pompilius, who

followed Romulus on the throne. Numa was renowned for introducing many religious cults and rituals to the Romans, and whereas Romulus was usually identified by the Romans with war, Numa was identified with religion.

641. caesa ... porca: abl. of means. The pig was a common sacrificial victim; its mention here, however, recalls the omen of the sow and her thirty piglets encountered by the Trojans earlier in Book 8 (81–85) and sacrificed by Aeneas to Juno.

642. Haud procul inde: again Vergil indicates simultaneously both the passage of time and the next scene on the shield. **Mettum**: the reference is to Mettus (sometimes called Mettius) Fufetius, a ruler of Alba Longa notorious for his treacherous abandonment of allies in battle and attempt to change sides. Livy 1.23–29 describes in some detail how Mett(i)us was drawn and quartered, and suggests that the punishment suited the crime.

642–43. in diversa ... distulerant: i.e., his body was torn apart by being pulled in different directions.

distulerant (at tu dictis, Albane, maneres!),
raptabatque viri mendacis viscera Tullus
per silvam, et sparsi rorabant sanguine vepres.//   645
Nec non Tarquinium eiectum Porsenna iubebat
accipere ingentique urbem obsidione premebat;
Aeneadae in ferrum pro libertate ruebant.
Illum indignanti similem similemque minanti

Aeneades, -ae, *m.* descendant of Aeneas

Albanus, -a, -um Alban, having to do with
the town of Alba

differo, differre, distuli, dilatus disperse,
separate, draw or tear apart

eicio, -ere, eieci, eiectus drive out, expel,
cast out

indignor (1) be angry, be indignant,
complain, protest

libertas, libertatis, *f.* freedom, liberty

mendax, mendacis given to lying,
mendacious, deceptive, lying

minor (1) threaten, menace

obsidio, obsidionis, *f.* siege, blockade

Porsenna, -ae, *m.* Lars Porsenna, a king of
Etruria who made war on Rome

rapto (1) snatch up, seize and carry off,
plunder, lay waste, drag

roro (1) let fall, drop, trickle, be dewy

Tarquinius, -i, *m.* Tarquinius Superbus,
last king of Rome

Tullus, -i, *m.* Tullus Hostilius, a king of
Rome

vepres, -ium, *m. pl.* thorn bush, brambles

viscus, visceris, *n.* innards, internal organs

---

643. **(at tu dictis, Albane, maneres!):**
Vergil's emotional APOSTROPHE marks the exceptional nature of Mett(i)us' treachery. **dictis:** dat. **maneres:** impf. subjunctive used to express both a contrary-to-fact protasis (i.e., Mett(i)us did not in fact stand by his word) and the speaker's unfulfilled wish that he had; sometimes called a "past jussive."

644. **viri mendacis:** i.e., Mett(i)us Fufetius. **Tullus:** i.e., Tullus Hostilius, the third king of Rome. This reference also marks the passage of time in the ECPHRASIS, since the scene just before this one evokes the eras of the two earlier kings, Romulus and Numa (see above, note on 640).

645. **sanguine:** another suggestion of color on the shield.

646. **Tarquinium eiectum:** the last of Rome's seven kings was Tarquinius Superbus, whose abuse of power provoked the wrath of the people of Rome. As the result of an uprising led by L. Iunius Brutus, Tarquinius (often called Tarquin in English) and his family were expelled from Rome and taken in by Lars Porsenna, king of the Etruscan settlement Clusium.

646–47. **Porsenna iubebat ... premebat:** the use of the impf. serves two purposes: it both characterizes Porsenna's behavior as frozen in time on the shield, and has conative force—i.e., it characterizes as continuous and/or repeated, but unsuccessful, Porsenna's attempt to reinstate Tarquinius. **accipere:** take with **iubebat;** the subject of the inf. is implied, probably = **suos,** i.e., the people of Clusium.

648. **Aeneadae:** like **Romulidis** (638) a Greek patronymic, Homeric in flavor. The relationship of Aeneas, the recipient and first viewer of the shield, to its subject matter is thus subtly reinforced. **in ferrum:** METONYMY for, e.g., **in bellum** or **in proelia.**

649. **Illum indignanti similem similemque minanti: illum** refers to Porsenna, whose attempt to reinstate Tarquinius was eventually thwarted by the characters whom we shall meet in the next two lines. The CHIASTIC arrangement of two pres. act. participles in the dat. (**indignanti, minanti**) and the repeated word **similem** is unusual and striking.

650   aspiceres, pontem auderet quia vellere Cocles
        et fluvium vinclis innaret Cloelia ruptis.
        In summo custos Tarpeiae Manlius arcis

Cloelia, -ae, *f.* Cloelia, Roman girl who
    swam the Tiber to escape from Porsenna
Cocles, Coclitis, *m.* Horatius Cocles,
    a Roman who defended a bridge by
    himself in the war against Porsenna
fluvius, -i, *m.* river
inno (1) swim in
Manlius, -i, *m.* M. Manlius Capitolinus, a
    Roman

pons, pontis, *m.* bridge
quia because, since
Tarpeius, -a, -um Tarpeian, a member of
    the *gens Tarpeia* or an epithet associated
    with one part of the Capitolium
vello, -ere, vulsi *or* **velli, vulsus** tear out,
    pull apart, tear down
vinc(u)lum, -i, *n.* chain, bond, fetter

---

650. **aspiceres:** for the second time (cf. 643) Vergil interrupts the third-person narrative of the shield with an address to a second person, in this case, the reader. The impf. subjunctive is used here to indicate potential, i.e., "you would have seen." **pontem auderet quia vellere Cocles:** note the postponement of the conjunction. **quia auderet:** impf. subjunctive in a clause dependent on the participles **indignanti** and **minanti.** The subjunctive indicates that the narrator is explaining Cocles' "daring" not from his own perspective but from that of Porsenna. **Cocles:** the heroism of Horatius Cocles in the face of an enemy attack is the subject of another tale preserved for us by Livy (Book 2.10). At the time of the battle between Tarquinius' supporters and the Romans, there existed a single bridge crossing the Tiber between the two groups. This bridge was therefore the obvious route for would-be assailants to take to besiege Rome. Recognizing this fact, Horatius placed himself at the end of the bridge opposite from the Roman side and

invited his comrades to destroy the bridge behind him, thus stranding himself. After killing numerous attackers, he jumped into the Tiber, offering himself as a sacrifice to safeguard Rome.

651. **innaret:** like **auderet** in the preceding line, impf. subjunctive is used here to suggest Porsenna's perspective, and looks back to the participles **indignanti** and **minanti. Cloelia:** subject of **innaret.** Cloelia's heroism is described by Livy shortly after the episode of Horatius Cocles (Book 2.13). An unmarried girl, Cloelia escaped with some of the hostages taken by Porsenna and swam across the Tiber; she later returned voluntarily and was rewarded by Porsenna's freeing of the others. **vinclis ... ruptis:** abl. abs.

652. **In summo:** Vergil again offers a suggestion for a scene's placement on the shield: at the top. A second interpretation is also possible, however: **in summo** may be construed with **Tarpeiae ... arcis,** i.e., "on the top of the Tarpeian citadel."

stabat pro templo et Capitolia celsa tenebat,
Romuleoque recens horrebat regia culmo.
Atque hic auratis volitans argenteus anser ~~goose~~   655
porticibus Gallos in limine adesse canebat;

---

anser, anseris, *m.* goose

argenteus, -a, -um silver, made from
   silver, silver-colored

auratus, -a, -um ornamented with gold,
   gilded

Capitolium, -i, *n.* the Capitoline hill, on
   which are located the citadel, the temple
   of Jupiter Optimus Maximus, and many
   other important temples and scenes of
   famous events in early Roman history

culmus, -i, *m.* stalk, stem, thatch

Gallus, -i, *m.* a Gaul

porticus, -us, *f.* colonnade, porch, portico

recens, recentis fresh, new, recent

regia, -ae, *f.* royal palace, residence

Romuleus, -a, -um of or belonging to
   Romulus

volito (1) flit about, flutter, fly

652–53. **custos ... Manlius**: M. Manlius Capitolinus received his cognomen from the fact that he lived on the Capitoline hill (**Capitolia celsa**), where he kept watch over the temples of Jupiter Optimus Maximus and Juno Moneta. When the Gauls attacked Rome c. 390 BCE, attempting to seize the citadel by stealth during the night, the geese sacred to Juno cackled and aroused Manlius, who was able to raise the alarm and so to save the city. Much of Livy Book 5 is devoted to this episode in Rome's history and its consequences. **Tarpeiae ... arcis**: The Capitoline hill has two major peaks, one of which was sometimes identified as the Tarpeian rock or citadel. The place-name recalls the girl Tarpeia, who fell in love at first sight with the Sabine king Titus Tatius (see above, 638) and decided to betray the city to him in hopes of winning his gratitude and love. Livy (Book 1.11) reports that, in one version of her story, when Tarpeia opened the gates to the Sabines, they rushed in; instead of thanking her, however, they piled their weapons on top of her and so crushed her to death to repay her treachery. Thereafter, the rock upon which she died was known as the Tarpeian rock, and criminals who had committed treason were thrown from it to their deaths.

653. **stabat ... tenebat**: the positioning of each verb at the beginning and end of the line reflects the defensive role of Manlius around the temples and citadel of the Capitoline.

654. **Romuleo ... horrebat ... culmo**: the dwelling of Rome's founder on the Capitoline was preserved by the Romans in its ancient state, complete with rough thatched roof, as an historic monument. We might compare the log cabin in which Abraham Lincoln was born and raised in Springfield, Illinois. It is also worth noting, however, that, like George Washington, Romulus appears to have slept in more than one place—another ancient hut identified with Romulus stood on the Palatine, adjacent to the site of Augustus' **domus. recens ... regia**: the noun recalls Romulus' role as first **rex**; its epithet is a reminder that Romulus had been king not very long before the attack of the Gauls (in fact, about 350 years previously).

655–56. **hic**: here, i.e., on the shield and on the Capitoline. **auratis ... porticibus**: the **porticus** of a temple is similar to a porch, an open-air space covered with a roof supported by columns. The earliest Roman temples were built primarily of wood, but were richly decorated with painted terracotta ornament. **argenteus anser**: a collective singular, indicating the geese in Juno's temple precinct. With the epithets **auratis** and **argenteus**, Vergil again suggests how colorful the shield is.

656. **Gallos in limine adesse**: indir. statement with **canebat. canebat**: a pleasing euphemism for the sound made by geese, that also suggests divine inspiration—i.e., the geese were divinely inspired to save Rome.

Mar.17/08

Galli per dumos aderant arcemque tenebant
defensi tenebris et dono noctis opacae. → *dative of possession.*
Aurea caesaries ollis atque aurea vestis,
660   virgatis lucent sagulis, tum lactea colla
auro innectuntur, duo quisque Alpina coruscant
gaesa manu, scutis protecti corpora longis. → *March 10*

Alpinus, -a, -um Alpine, having to do
   with the Alps

caesaries, -ei, *f.* hair

collum, -i, *n.* neck

corusco (1) brandish, wave, shake

defendo, -ere, defendi, defensus defend

dumus, -i, *m.* thorn-bush, bramble

duo, duae, duo two

gaesum, -i, *n.* long, heavy javelin of the
   Gauls

innecto, -ere, innexui, innexus fasten,
   garland, surround

lacteus, -a, -um milky, milk-white

luceo, -ere, luxi be bright, shine, gleam

opacus, -a, -um dark

protego, -ere, protexi, protectus cover,
   protect

quisque, quaeque, quodque each, every
   one

sagulum, -i, *n.* military cloak

scutum, -i, *n.* shield

tenebrae, -arum, *f.* darkness, shadow,
   darkness of night

virgatus, -a, -um striped

---

657. **per dumos**: cf. **vepres** (645). Vergil
depicts early Rome as a wilderness, not yet
fully civilized.

658. **defensi tenebris et dono noctis
opacae**: night as a time for treachery is a re-
curring motif in the *Aeneid*: cf. the episodes
involving the Trojan horse in Book 2 and
Nisus and Euryalus in Book 9.

659–61. **Aurea … aurea … auro**: the
threefold repetition of references to gold in
the appearance and equipment of the Gauls
suggests that they stand out vividly on the
shield; cf. also **lucent** and **lactea. ollis**: an
archaic form, equivalent to **illis. tum**: here,
has the relatively unusual meaning "in
addition," "besides." **virgatis … sagulis**:
the detailed depiction of the Gauls' cloth-
ing helps to identify them as non-Roman.

lactea colla auro innectuntur: the Gauls
traditionally wore solid gold necklaces, or
torques, and are so depicted frequently in
ancient sculpture.

661–62. **duo … Alpina … gaesa**: neut. pl.
acc. obj. of **coruscant**; the javelins are said
to be Alpine because the Alps separate Gaul
from Italy, and the Gauls had to cross them
in their march on Rome. They are likely to
have used the wood from Alpine trees to
make their javelins. **quisque** is nom. singu-
lar, but is used distributively with a plural
verb: "each and every one of them bran-
dishes …." **protecti corpora**: the perf. pass.
participle used with the so-called Greek acc.
corpora, lit., "covered by long shields with
respect to their bodies," i.e., having covered
their bodies with their long shields.

Hic exsultantes Salios nudosque Lupercos
lanigerosque apices et lapsa ancilia caelo
extuderat, castae ducebant sacra per urbem   665
pilentis matres in mollibus. Hinc procul addit

---

ancile, ancilis, *n.* figure-eight shield

apex, apicis, *m.* peak, top, cap

castus, -a, -um chaste, upright, moral

exsulto (1) jump, leap

extundo, -ere, extudi, extusus hammer, produce with effort, emboss

laniger, lanigera, lanigerum wool-bearing, fleecy

Lupercus, -i, *m.* priest of Lycaean Pan

mollis, -e soft, gentle

nudus, -a, -um naked, nude

pilentum, -i, *n.* easy chariot or carriage

Salii, -orum, *m. pl.* Salii, priests dedicated to the service of Mars

---

663. **Hic**: the description of the next scene on the shield begins. **exsultantes Salios**: the first in a series of four dir. objs. of **extuderat** (665). The Salii were priests of Mars, whose worship included dancing and leaping; their name is derived from the verb **salio, salire,** "to jump," and the participle **exsultantes** is a pun on their name. **nudosque Lupercos**: the Luperci were priests of Pan (also known in Latin as Faunus), and celebrated their god every February during the festival of Lupercalia. In this festival, which emphasized the importance of childbearing to sustain the manpower of Rome, the Luperci ran along a processional route through Rome, wearing only leather loincloths (thus Vergil calls them **nudi**), and flicking long strips of leather at the crowds as they ran by. Newly wed women in particular were eager to be touched by the lash, since they believed that this would improve their fertility.

664. **lanigerosque apices**: the unusual dress of the Salii is described: each of them wore a special cap consisting of a wooden disc topped with a tuft of wool. The compound adj. **lanigeros**, referring to this tuft, adds to the solemnity of the scene with its epic flavor. **lapsa ancilia caelo**: the ritual dance of the Salii commemorated the de-

scent from the sky of a divinely made **ancile**, or figure-eight shield, interpreted by Numa as a sign of Roman authority. Eleven copies of the original **ancile** were made, and all were kept in the **regia**, so that the original could not be identified and thus stolen or destroyed. Vergil thus incorporates a scene concerning one divinely crafted shield into his description of a second divinely crafted shield. **caelo** is abl. of place from which; the preposition (**de** or **ex**) has been omitted.

665. **extuderat**: after the relatively colorless **fecerat** (630) and **addiderat** (637), this verb underscores Mars' effort in crafting so exceptional a shield.

665–66. **castae ... matres**: the married women of Rome, who were rewarded with the honor of riding in special cushioned wagons (**pilentis ... in mollibus**) in return for their pious efforts on behalf of Rome during the Gallic siege.

666. **Hinc procul**: the next scene chronologically is far separated spatially on the shield from those that preceded it. **addit**: roughly equivalent to **addiderat**, although the sudden use of the pres. tense also serves as a reminder that the historical sequence of scenes on the shield is approaching the present, that is, the present from the perspective of Vergil and his first readers.

Tartareas etiam sedes, alta ostia Ditis,
et scelerum poenas et te, Catilina, minaci
pendentem scopulo Furiarumque ora trementem,
670   secretosque pios, his dantem iura Catonem. ⏐

Catilina, -ae, *m.* L. Sergius Catilina, leader of a conspiracy against the Roman state during the consulship of Cicero

Cato, -onis, *m.* M. Porcius Cato, Roman consul and censor

Dis, Ditis, *m.* Dis, ruler of the underworld; also known as Pluto(n)

Furiae, -arum, *f. pl.* the Furies, goddesses of vengeance

ius, iuris, *n.* law

minax, minacis threatening, menacing

ostium, -i, *n.* door, entrance

scelus, sceleris, *n.* crime

secretus, -a, -um existing apart, separate from, set apart

Tartareus, -a, -um Tartarean, of or having to do with the underworld

---

667. **Tartareas ... sedes**: the underworld was sometimes identified with the monster Tartarus, and sometimes, as here, called his home. **etiam**: suggests the great distance between this and the previous scene, as the shield's imagery extends to the very depths of Tartarus. **alta ostia**: in apposition to **sedes**. **Ditis**: the god who presided over the underworld was identified ironically with wealth (cf. **dives, divitiae**) since he was the ruler of so many dead. His Latin name is a translation of his Greek name, Pluto/Ploutos (wealth).

668. **et te, Catilina**: for the third time in the ECPHRASIS, Vergil employs dir. address, here APOSTROPHIZING L. Sergius Catilina, the noble but dissolute and disaffected Roman who in 63 BCE made an unsuccessful attempt to overthrow the government; his prime target, the distinguished orator Marcus Tullius Cicero, one of the two consuls that year, discovered the plot (including a plan to assassinate him) and delivered a series of speeches (*In Catilinam* 1–4, the first of which was delivered from the steps of the temple of Jupiter Stator: see above, note on 640) which helped to bring Catilina down and to stabilize the republic.

669. **pendentem ... trementem**: the combination of APOSTROPHE and pres. act. participles helps to increase the vividness of the scene. **Furiarumque ora**: the three Furies, female personifications of revenge, were renowned in myth for their horrific appearance.

670. **secretosque pios**: both of these epithets create a sharp contrast to the preceding scene; pious and law-abiding men are set far apart from the criminals in the underworld. **his**: refers to **secretosque pios**. **Catonem**: the younger Cato, M. Porcius Cato Uticensis, a conservative defender of republican Roman values and staunch opponent of Catilina; during Catilina's trial, Cato argued for the death penalty. Cato was also an opponent of Julius Caesar.

671–713. With the last reference to Catilina and Cato, Vergil has brought the scenes in the ECPHRASIS close to his own era; and the juxtaposition of these two men, one depicted as treacherous criminal and the other as quasi-divine hero, anticipates the portraits of Antony and Augustus in the culminating scene.

The ensuing scene is central to the shield in many ways: its description alone fills 39 of 103 total lines in the ECPHRASIS, and numerous details in Vergil's description ensure that the scene is clearly set off from the others and given central position. The subject is the battle of Actium, the final confrontation of two former friends now turned mortal enemies. In 42 BCE, Antony had gone to the East in his capacity as Octavian's partner in sharing control of the Roman world; there he renewed an earlier acquaintance with the Macedonian queen of Egypt Cleopatra VII, and was said to have fallen hopelessly in love with her. They had three children together, and Antony decided to include them in his will. Back in Rome, Octavian took advantage of this decision and popularized an image of Antony as traitor to Roman traditions.

> Haec inter tumidi late maris ibat imago
> aurea, sed fluctu spumabant caerula cano,
> et circum argento clari delphines in orbem
> aequora verrebant caudis aestumque secabant.
> In medio classes aeratas, Actia bella,   675

Actius, -a, -um Actian, of or having to do with Actium

aeratus, -a, -um decorated with bronze, brazen

aestus, -us, *m.* tide, current, sea; heat

argentum, -i, *n.* silver

caerul(e)us, -a, -um blue, greenish blue; celestial

canus, -a, -um white, whitened

cauda, -ae, *f.* tail

delphin, delphinis, *m.* dolphin

late *adv.* far and wide, broadly

seco, -are, secui, sectus cut, divide

tumidus, -a, -um swollen

verro, -ere sweep, pass over (a surface)

---

671. Haec inter: a reversal of the usual word order is ANASTROPHE.

671–72. imago *aurea,* **fluctu** ... *cano,* **spumabant** *caerula:* no fewer than three colors stand out in Mars' depiction of the stirred-up sea. **caerula:** here used as a substantive.

673. argento: abl. of material or of description with **clari. delphines:** dolphins were associated with Apollo, whom Augustus considered his special patron. Note that the nom. pl. ending (-es) of this Greek noun is a short syllable, retaining its quantity from Greek. **in orbem:** the pattern of the dolphins' swimming imposes control on the image of the otherwise wild waters.

675. In medio: i.e., in the center of the shield, and in the middle of the ECPHRASIS (49 lines precede and 51 lines follow 675–77). **classes aeratas, Actia bella:** the second phrase is in apposition to the first, and the two are arranged CHIASTICALLY. **aeratas:** in addition to describing the material of the shield upon which this scene is embossed, this epithet alludes to the ships' *rostra,* bronze battering rams that were used offensively to damage enemy ships. Cf. also note on 684. **Actia:** the adj. is derived from the place-name Actium, a promontory located on the west cost of the Greek mainland famous for its temple of Apollo.

cernere erat, totumque instructo Marte videres
fervere Leucaten auroque effulgere fluctus.
Hinc Augustus agens Italos in proelia Caesar
cum patribus populoque, penatibus et magnis dis,
680   stans celsa in puppi, geminas cui tempora flammas

Augustus, -i, *m.* Augustus, honorific title assumed by Octavian in 27 BCE

Caesar, Caesaris, *m.* Caesar, the *cognomen* used by members of one branch of the *gens Iulia*; after Augustus' reign, *Caesar* becomes an honorific title for all succeeding Roman emperors

effulgo, -ere, effulsi blaze forth, flash, gleam

ferveo, -ere, fervi boil

instruo, -ere, instruxi, instructus construct, draw up (in a battle formation)

Italus, -a, -um Italian, having to do with Italy

Leucate, -es, *f.* promontory on southern side of the island of Leucas

Mars, Martis, *m.* Mars, god of war

pater, patris, *m.* father; senator

Penates, -ium, *m. pl.* gods of the household and of the Roman state

proelium, -i, *n.* battle

tempus, temporis, *n.* side of the forehead, temple

---

676. **cernere erat**: i.e., **cerni poterat. instructo Marte**: lit., Mars having been drawn up (i.e., for battle); **Mars** is a METONYMY for the lines of soldiers preparing to fight. **videres**: past potential impf. For the third time in the ECPHRASIS Vergil addresses his reader directly, and so enhances the vividness of his description while drawing attention to its visual illusion.

677. **fervĕre ... effulgĕre**: note that the stem-vowel -e- in each of these archaic third conjugation forms of the inf. is a short syllable; these infs. are used in indir. statement after **videres. fervere** suggests that the place of battle was boiling with turmoil—an effect that would in fact be very difficult to depict or to see on the shield. **Leucaten**: Greek acc. Leucas was the name of an island off the south coast of Actium; its chief city, with its own temple of Apollo, was Leucate. **auro**: abl. of material.

678. **Hinc**: i.e., on one side of the scene; further directional signals for visualizing this scene are given in 682 (**Parte alia**) and 685 (**Hinc**). This particular scene (678–81)

is at the very center of the description of the scenes on the shield (48 + 4 + 47 lines). **Augustus ... Caesar**: emphatic placement. At the time of the battle of Actium, Octavian had not yet assumed the cognomen Augustus; he did so only in 27 BCE. Vergil, however, anticipates in his description an event that must have been very fresh in the memories of his first readers.

679. **cum patribus populoque, penatibus et magnis dis**: the entire line is used to describe four distinct entities who lend Augustus their support (either physical or symbolic, or both). The arrangement is CHIASTIC, with the two elite groups (**patribus ... et magnis dis**) enclosing the two humble sources of support (**populo, penatibus**).

680. **geminas ... flammas**: dir. obj. of **vomunt** (681). The depiction of flames on the head as a sign of divine favor recalls earlier scenes with Iulus (2.682–91) and Lavinia (7.71–80). **cui**: i.e., Augustus; dat. of reference, here related to dat. of possession; translate as **illi**, i.e., "his."

laeta vomunt patriumque aperitur vertice sidus.
Parte alia ventis et dis Agrippa secundis
arduus agmen agens, cui, belli insigne superbum,
tempora navali fulgent rostrata corona.
Hinc ope barbarica variisque Antonius armis,   685

Agrippa, -ae, *m.* M. Vipsanius Agrippa,
friend and general of Augustus

Antonius, -i, *m.* Marcus Antonius (often
called Antony or Marc Antony in
English)

barbaricus, -a, -um barbarian, foreign

corona, -ae, *f.* crown

fulgeo, -ere, fulsi shine, gleam

navalis, -e naval, nautical

rostratus, -a, -um beaked

tempus, temporis, *n.* side of the forehead,
temple

vertex, verticis, *m.* top of the head, crown

vomo, -ere, vomui, vomitus discharge,
spew, pour forth, emit

---

681. **patrium ... sidus:** i.e., the star em-
bodying Julius Caesar, Augustus' adoptive
father. The image evokes a popular belief
that, during his funeral, Julius Caesar's
ascent to divine status was marked by the
appearance of a comet or shooting star; de-
pictions of Caesar with a star on his head
appeared in statues and on coins. **aperitur:**
i.e., is revealed.

682. **Parte alia:** i.e., in another part of
the scene; cf. 678 and 685. **ventis et dis ...
secundis:** the adj. is shared by both nouns.
Agrippa: M. Vipsanius Agrippa, friend, col-
league, and eventual son-in-law of Augus-
tus. Agrippa commanded Octavian's fleet
throughout the 30s BCE, and other historical
sources suggest that he led the Romans at
Actium. After the death of Marcellus (see
Book 6.860–86), Augustus arranged for the
marriage of his daughter Julia to Agrippa;
Julia and Agrippa had several children,
the two eldest of whom, Gaius and Lucius,
were adopted by Augustus as his heirs.
Agrippa died in 12 BCE.

683. **arduus agmen agens:** the use of two
adjs. without a conjunction (e.g., **et**) is un-
usual and striking; cf. Book 12.897. **arduus**
may be most easily translated with an ad-
verbial phrase, "on high." **cui:** i.e., Agrippa;
dat. of reference, here related to dat. of pos-
session. **belli insigne superbum:** in appo-
sition (not entirely logically) to **tempora** in
the next line.

684. The word order seen in this line (5
words, including a central verb and two
epithet-noun phrases distributed on either
side) has the modern name GOLDEN LINE.
(Dryden first used the term.) **tempora:** the
attention given to Agrippa's forehead par-
allels that given to Octavian's (above, 680).
navali ... corona: the **corona navalis** was
an honorary crown given as a mark of dis-
tinction to the victorious general in a sea
battle; as the perf. pass. participle **rostrata**
indicates, the crown was decorated with
miniature replicas of the ships' beaks, or
rostra, taken in battle. Agrippa was award-
ed this honor in 36 BCE.

685. **Hinc:** the third directional adv. or
phrase in this battle scene. **ope barbarica:**
in Roman thought it was something of a
cliché that the peoples living in the eastern
Mediterranean enjoyed lives of excessive,
even degenerate luxury. The epithet **bar-
barica**, from the Greek word for "foreign-
er," is a striking device to turn the reader's
attention to Antony. **variis ... armis:** the ep-
ithet not only refers to the various groups
of men under Antony's command, but also
suggests the variegated colors of their gar-
ments. **Antonius:** Marcus Antonius, former
colleague of Octavian but now portrayed as
an enemy not only of his old friend but of
the state.

victor ab Aurorae populis et litore rubro,
Aegyptum viresque Orientis et ultima secum
Bactra vehit, sequiturque (nefas) Aegyptia coniunx.
Una omnes ruere ac totum spumare reductis
690   convulsum remis rostrisque tridentibus aequor.
Alta petunt; pelago credas innare revulsas
Cycladas aut montes concurrere montibus altos,

Aegyptius, -a, -um Egyptian

Aegyptus, -i, f. Egypt

Aurora, -ae, f. the East, the Orient

Bactra, -orum, n. pl. the province of Bactra, in ancient Parthia

concurro, -ere, concurri, concursus run together, charge

coniunx, coniugis, m./f. partner, wife, husband, consort

convello, -ere, convelli, convulsus pull violently, batter, shatter

credo, -ere, credidi, creditus believe

Cyclas, Cycladis, f. one of the Cyclades islands, near Delos

inno (1) swim in

nefas, n. (*indecl.*) crime (lit., unspeakable thing)

Oriens, Orientis, m. the Orient

reduco, -ere, reduxi, reductus lead back, draw back

revello, -ere, revelli, revulsus tear loose, tear up

rostrum, -i, n. beak of a ship

ruber, rubra, rubrum red, reddish

tridens, tridentis having three prongs

ultimus, -a, -um farthest, most distant

veho, -ere, vexi, vectus carry, convey, transport

---

686. **victor**: used ironically, since Antony's campaign in Parthia (36 bce) was hardly worth celebrating, and he was defeated at Actium. **Aurorae**: a geographical metonymy, since dawn rises in the east. **litore rubro**: the Indian ocean, called "red" here because of the east's association with sunrise.

687–88. **Aegyptum ... Bactra**: Antony's followers come not only from Egypt but from distant India. **vires Orientis**: like **Aurorae** in the preceding line, **Orientis** alludes to the place where the sun rises.

688. **nefas**: in apposition to **Aegyptia coniunx**, but usually punctuated as a parenthetical exclamation, anticipating Vergil's avoidance of her proper name. The literal meaning of **nefas**, from ne + fari, is "not speakable." **Aegyptia coniunx**: Cleopatra; but Vergil, like all the other Augustan poets, never calls her by her proper name.

689. **una**: adverbial. **ruere ... spumare**: historical infs.

690. **rostrisque tridentibus**: a bronze *rostrum* typically has three prongs.

691. **credas**: Vergil addresses the reader for the fourth time in the ecphrasis; the pres. potential subjunctive used here (as opposed to the impf. subjunctives earlier) strives for increased vividness in this climactic scene.

691–92. **innare ... concurrere**: infs. in indir. statement after **credas**. **revulsas Cycladas**: Vergil invites his reader to visualize an event which could in fact happen only as the result of a cataclysmic natural occurrence, like an earthquake or tidal wave. The Cyclades are a chain of small islands lying in the Aegean sea southeast of mainland Greece.

tanta mole viri turritis puppibus instant.
Stuppea flamma manu telisque volatile ferrum
spargitur, arva nova Neptunia caede rubescunt.   695
Regina in mediis patrio vocat agmina sistro,
necdum etiam geminos a tergo respicit angues.

---

anguis, -is, *m.* snake, serpent
caedes, -is, *f.* slaughter, bloodshed
insto, -are, institi press on, assail
moles, -is, *f.* great mass, pile
necdum and not yet
Neptunius, -a, -um of or having to do with
    Neptune

rubesco, -ere, rubui become red, redden
sistrum, -i, *n.* rattle, used in worship of Isis
stuppeus, -a, -um made of tow, hempen
turritus, -a, -um turreted, having towers
volatilis, -e able to fly, flying

---

693. **turritis puppibus:** Roman battle-
ships typically had one or two towers on
the deck, from which missiles (e.g., spears)
could be thrown or hurled.

694. **Stuppea flamma manu telisque
volatile ferrum:** note the CHIASTIC arrange-
ment: nom. adj./noun pair – abl. noun – abl.
noun – nom. adj./noun pair. A typical strat-
egy in a sea battle would involve ramming
an enemy's ship with the *rostrum* of one's
own ship, and so preventing the enemy
from escaping. Then, with the enemy's
ship held close by the *rostrum,* one's troops
could fight at close range, throwing both
conventional weapons and flaming rope at
the trapped opponent.

695. **spargitur:** a sing. verb is used even
though it has two subjects (**flamma** and **fer-
rum**) because the subject mentioned closer
to the verb is sing. **arva ... Neptunia:** the
image inverts usual expectations: Vergil
describes the sea running with blood as if
it were a field being plowed. The basis of
the similarity is not made explicit by Ver-
gil, but is probably linked to the parallel
between plowing the earth (= tearing or

cutting through the surface of the soil) and
the cutting of the sea by ships' prows. **ru-
bescunt:** color again is emphasized.

696. **Regina:** Cleopatra. **in mediis:** i.e.,
aequoribus or **viris;** but an inherent am-
biguity allows readers to interpret this
phrase as directing the viewer to a location
on the shield. **patrio sistro:** the **sistrum** is
a hand-held rattle made of bronze. Its men-
tion typically evokes the cult of the Egyp-
tian goddess Isis, since her worshippers are
regularly depicted holding a **sistrum.** The
suggestion that Cleopatra is like Isis re-
flects both the queen's importance and her
semi-divine status.

697. **necdum etiam ... respicit:** Vergil
suggests that she is depicted in the brief
moments before she sees her destiny ap-
proaching. **geminos ... angues:** the twin
snakes here recall the pairing of Octavian
and Agrippa as Antony's (and Cleopatra's)
rivals earlier in this scene. This unantici-
pated attack of twin snakes should also
be compared with that at Book 2.201–27. **a
tergo:** i.e., from behind, and so, unseen.

Omnigenumque deum monstra et latrator Anubis
contra Neptunum et Venerem contraque Minervam
700   tela tenent. Saevit medio in certamine Mavors
caelatus ferro, tristesque ex aethere Dirae,
et scissa gaudens vadit Discordia palla,
quam cum sanguineo sequitur Bellona flagello.⟩

Anubis, -is, *m.* Anubis, Egyptian god with the body of a man and the head of a dog

Bellona, -ae, *f.* Bellona, goddess of war

caelo (1) emboss, engrave, chisel

Dirae, -arum, *f.* the Dirae, Italian goddesses associated with the Furies

Discordia, -ae, *f.* Discord, Disagreement

flagellum, -i, *n.* whip, lash

gaudeo, -ere, gavisus sum rejoice, delight, take pleasure in

latrator, latratoris, *m.* barker, one who barks

Mavors, Mavortis, *m.* Mars, god of war

Minerva, -ae, *f.* Minerva, goddess of wisdom and the arts

Neptunus, -i, *m.* Neptune, god of the sea

omnigenus, -a, -um of every kind

palla, -ae, *f.* mantle, robe, cloak

saevio, -ire, saevii rage, act savagely

sanguineus, -a, -um bloody

scindo, -ere, scicidi *or* **scidi, scissus** tear, rend

vado, -ere proceed, go

Venus, Veneris, *f.* Venus, goddess of love and beauty

---

698. **Omnigenumque deum**: gen. pl. The adj. is a compound modeled on a Greek compound; the **-um** ending is an archaic alternative for **-orum**. Vergil alludes to the fact that, unlike the divinities of the Greeks and Romans, many Egyptian gods were not human in form, but animals or part-animal, part-human combinations. **latrator Anubis**: Anubis has the body of a man and the head of a dog, and so is described here as the "barker."

698–99. The first of these lines is devoted to Egyptian gods, the second, to their Roman opponents. Vergil suggests that the gods themselves fight on behalf of their worshippers, and thus that the battle of Actium has religious and cultural implications as well as political ones.

700. **medio in certamine**: note the word order. With the first two words in the phrase, Vergil appears to be directing us again to the placement of the characters on the shield; but as **certamine** shows, he is locating Mars on the battlefield itself. **Mavors**: archaic form of Mars; see 630, above.

701. **caelatus ferro**: describes Mars; the placement of the phrase in ENJAMBMENT serves to remind the reader that the scene just described is a picture, rather than an actual battle. **ferro**: abl. of material. **tristes … Dirae**: the Dirae are Italian divinities related to the Furies. The adj. describes both their grim appearance and the effect they have on others. **ex aethere**: i.e., descending from above (cf. Venus' descent above and note on 608).

702. **scissa … palla**: abl. abs. The **palla** is a mantle typically worn by a woman; its tearing signifies a profound breakdown in civilized behavior. **gaudens**: juxtaposed with **scissa**, creates a vivid OXYMORON. **Discordia**: the PERSONIFICATION of discord, whose association with the Dirae goes back to Ennius.

703. **quam**: i.e., Discordia. **cum sanguineo … flagello**: the epithet alludes both to the events of war and to the colors visible on the shield. **Bellona**: an Italian goddess of war, here depicted as an attendant to Discordia.

Actius haec cernens arcum intendebat Apollo
desuper; omnis eo terrore Aegyptus et Indi,   705
omnis Arabs, omnes vertebant terga Sabaei.
Ipsa videbatur ventis regina vocatis
vela dare et laxos iam iamque immittere funes.
Illam inter caedes pallentem morte futura
fecerat ignipotens undis et Iapyge ferri,   710

Actius, -a, -um Actian, of or having to do
   with Actium

Aegyptus, -i, f. Egypt

Apollo, Apollinis, m. Apollo, god of
   music, prophecy, archery and medicine

Arabs, Arabis, m. an Arab, inhabitant of
   Arabia

arcus, -us, m. bow

caedes, -is, f. slaughter, bloodshed

desuper adv. from above

funis, -is, m. rope, cable

Iapyx, Iapygis, m. Iapyx, the northwest
   wind

ignipotens, -ntis potent in fire, ruler of
   fire, powerful in fire

immitto, -ere, immisi, immissus release,
   let loose

Indus, -i, m. inhabitant of India

laxus, -a, -um loose, slack

pallens, pallentis pale, pallid

Sabaeus, -a, -um Sabaean, of or from
   Arabia

terror, terroris, m. fear, terror; person or
   thing that creates terror

---

704. **Actius ... Apollo**: there was a
sanctuary of Apollo at Actium. Augustus
claimed that Apollo was his patron, and
saw his victory at Actium as a sign of Apollo's special favor. **haec cernens**: cf. **cernere
erat** in 676.

705. **desuper**: for a god entering the scene
from above, see the notes on 608 and 701.

705–6. **omnis ... Aegyptus**: effectively
adjectival, denoting each and every Egyptian. **eo terrore**: abl. of cause; = **eius terrore**,
i.e., with fear before this one. **Indi**: nom.
pl. after the generic nom. sing. **Aegyptus**;
the variation is not unusual. **omnis Arabs**:
nom. sing. **omnes ... Sabaei**: like **Indi** in
the preceding line, the second ethnic group
named here is in the nom. pl. The parallel
structure of the two lines, combined with
the ANAPHORA and ASYNDETON emphasizing
omnis/omnes, suggests that **omnes** is to be
understood with **Indi** as well.

707. **Ipsa ... regina**: Cleopatra. **ventis ...
vocatis**: abl. abs.

708. **vela dare et laxos ... immittere funes**: both **vela dare** and **immittere funes**
are sailing idioms: "to set sail" and "to let
loose the ropes"; take both infs. as complementary with **videbatur** in the preceding
line. **iam iamque**: suggests that she is depicted as just about to do these things, but
that she has not done them yet.

709–10. **Illam ... pallentem**: acc. subject of **ferri** in an infinitival construction
introduced by **fecerat** (cf. 630). **pallentem**
suggests more color on the shield. **morte
futura**: PROLEPTIC, predicting her death but
not showing it. Did Aeneas understand the
significance of her pallor when he looked
at the shield? **ignipotens**: cf. 628. **Iapyge**:
Iapyx is the name given to the northwest
wind (i.e., blowing from Italy); here it
serves as a METONYMY for wind. **ferri**: pres.
act. inf. in indir. statement: "...that she was
being borne ..."

contra autem magno maerentem corpore Nilum
pandentemque sinus et tota veste vocantem
caeruleum in gremium latebrosaque flumina victos.

---

caerul(e)us, -a, -um blue, greenish blue;
  celestial
gremium, -i, *n.* lap, bosom
latebrosus, -a, -um hidden, secret

maereo, -ere mourn, grieve
Nilus, -i, *m.* Nile river
sinus, -us, *m.* fold (of a garment), hollow,
  curve

711–13. **contra autem**: strongly adversative, suggesting that the following scene is diametrically opposed—both on the shield and symbolically—to the depiction of Cleopatra just given. **magno maerentem corpore Nilum**: SYNCHYSIS. **maerentem … Nilum**: PERSONIFICATION, enhanced by the reference to the Nile's body (**corpore**). In the next two lines, this personification is fully developed by references to the Nile's clothing and his lap, as well as his voice. **maerentem … pandentem … vocantem**: the pres. act. participles suggest that the depiction of the Nile on the shield actually seems to move.

713. **caeruleum in gremium latebrosaque flumina**: the two nouns and their respective epithets are acc. with **in**, expressing motion toward. The picture given here of the Nile recalls the depiction of the Tiber in the opening of Book 7. **caeruleum**: another color is suggested. **victos**: acc. dir. obj. of **vocantem**, referring to Antony, Cleopatra, and the surviving members of their army.

714–28. The final scene on the shield described by Vergil is the triumph of Octavian (here called Caesar) after the battle of Actium. Vergil does not indicate where this scene is located on the shield; perhaps it is to be imagined as centrally located between the scenes depicting the death of Cleopatra and the personified Nile, both representing defeat.

In 29 BCE Octavian celebrated a triple triumph, honoring his victories at Actium and over Illyricum and Egypt. One day of the triumph was dedicated to each of the three victories; the ceremony thus extended over three days. A **triumphator** was granted the right to have a triumphal procession within the walls of Rome to display both his vast military resources and the booty that he had won from his conquered opponent; this procession wound slowly throughout the center of the city, finishing before the temple of Jupiter Optimus Maximus on the Capitoline. The **triumphator** was considered on that day to be the human personification of Jupiter Optimus Maximus himself.

At Caesar, triplici invectus Romana triumpho
moenia, dis Italis votum immortale sacrabat,   715
maxima ter centum totam delubra per urbem.

Caesar, Caesaris, *m.* Caesar, the *cognomen* used by members of one branch of the *gens Iulia*; after Augustus' reign, *Caesar* becomes an honorific title for all succeeding Roman emperors
delubrum, -i, *n.* shrine, temple
immortalis, -e immortal, undying
inveho, -ere, invexi, invectus carry in(to), bring in(to)

Italus, -a, -um Italian, having to do with Italy
Romanus, -a, -um Roman, having to do with Rome
triplex, triplicis threefold, triple
triumphus, -i, *m.* triumph, triumphal procession
votum, -i, *n.* vow, offering

---

714. **At**: strongly adversative, directing our attention to a new scene (cf. note on 608). **Caesar**: Octavius was adopted by Julius Caesar posthumously, i.e., by means of Julius Caesar's will, in 44 BCE. In accordance with custom, Octavius' name was then changed to reflect his new status, and became **Gaius Iulius Caesar Octavianus**. The first three of these names replicate those of his new adoptive father; the last indicates that he had been born the son of Octavius, but was later adopted into another family (note the change from Octavius to Octavianus.) After his adoption, Octavianus (usually shortened in English to Octavian) received no other names until 27 BCE, when he added an honorific to his name. At that point, he became **Gaius Iulius Caesar Octavianus Augustus**, frequently abbreviated

as Caesar Augustus or Augustus Caesar. Thus, the reference to Caesar here is simply a shortened form of Octavian's name. **triplici … triumpho**: the triple triumph of 29 BCE. **invectus**: the passive form of this verb functions as a Greek middle, and so takes a dir. obj. (**Romana … moenia**).

716. **maxima ter centum … delubra**: the large round number is probably an exaggeration, since in his *Res Gestae* (20) Augustus himself mentions only 82 restored temples; other sources indicate that an additional 12 new temples were founded by Augustus. The large multiple of three recalls, among other things, the number of piglets (30) that Tiber had predicted would be seen being suckled by a sow upon Aeneas' arrival in Latium (8.42–48).

Laetitia ludisque viae plausuque fremebant;
omnibus in templis matrum chorus, omnibus arae;
ante aras terram caesi stravere iuvenci.

720   Ipse sedens niveo candentis limine Phoebi
dona recognoscit populorum aptatque superbis
postibus; incedunt victae longo ordine gentes,
quam variae linguis, habitu tam vestis et armis. ⎰ March 31ˢᵗ.

---

caedo, -ere, cecidi, caesus cut down, kill, slaughter

candens, candentis shining, gleaming

chorus, -i, *m.* chorus, group of people, group of worshippers

fremo, -ere, fremui, fremitus roar, rumble

habitus, -us, *m.* style, fashion, custom

incedo, -ere, incessi proceed, walk, step

iuvencus, -i, *m.* bull, ox, cattle

laetitia, -ae, *f.* happiness, joy

lingua, -ae, *f.* tongue; language

ludus, -i, *m.* game, sport

niveus, -a, -um snow-white, snowy

Phoebus, -i, *m.* another name for Apollo

plausus, -us, *m.* applause, approval

postis, -is, *m.* door-post

recognosco, -ere, recognovi, recognitus acknowledge, give recognition to

sterno, -ere, stravi, stratus lay down, stretch out on the ground, lay low

---

717. **Laetitia ludisque ... plausuque**: abl. of means.

718. **omnibus in templis ... , omnibus**: the combination of ANAPHORA and ASYNDETON indicates that **in templis** should also be understood with the second **omnibus**. Supply **erant** with both subjects.

719. **stravere = straverunt**. Vergil's style of expression here is unusual; with **iuvenci** as subject, it would be natural to expect a passive verb. Instead, **terram** serves as dir. obj.: "the cattle stretched out and covered the ground."

720. **Ipse**: i.e., Octavian. **niveo candentis limine Phoebi**: the use of SYNCHYSIS allows Vergil to juxtapose the nearly synonymous adjectives **niveo** and **candentis**. Vergil is probably also alluding to the etymology of Apollo's epithet **Phoebus**, which in Greek means "shining" or bright." This combination underscores the brilliant whiteness of the new temple to Actian Apollo, built by Octavian on the Palatine. Octavian used only the finest and most precious materials in the construction of this temple, and its marble was visible from on high throughout much of the city. The temple, together with its beautiful covered portico and libraries,

was immediately adjacent to Octavian's own house on the Palatine (which in turn was adjacent to one of the ancestral huts of Romulus; see above, note on 654). Yet its mention here as the site for Octavian's review of his own triumph is anachronistic: while vowed in 36 BCE, the temple was not dedicated until 28 BCE.

721. **dona recognoscit populorum**: in the triumphal procession, representatives of the conquered peoples would take part in the procession, carrying some of the booty taken from them and presenting it to the triumphant general as a "gift."

721–22. **aptatque superbis postibus**: typically a triumphant general would leave some of the spoils won in war hanging in or on the temple of Jupiter Capitolinus; here, however, Octavian dedicates them to Apollo in his new temple.

722. **victae ... gentes**: i.e., representatives of the conquered peoples.

723. **quam variae ... tam**: translate the correlatives with "as ... , as ... , " both modifying **variae**: "as varied in ... as in ..." **variae**: nom. pl., modifying **gentes. linguis, habitu, armis**: abl. of respect, with **variae**. **vestis**: gen. sing. with **habitu**.

Hic Nomadum genus et discinctos Mulciber Afros,
hic Lelegas Carasque sagittiferosque Gelonos   725
finxerat; Euphrates ibat iam mollior undis,
extremique hominum Morini, Rhenusque bicornis,
indomitique Dahae, et pontem indignatus Araxes.

Afer, Afra, Afrum African, of or having to do with Africa

Araxes, -is, *m.* Aras river

bicornis, -e two-horned

Car, Caris, *m.* Carian, inhabitant of Caria

Dahae, -arum, *m. pl.* the Dahae, a Scythian tribe

discinctus, -a, -um ungirt, unbelted

Euphrates, -i, *m.* Euphrates river

Geloni, -orum, *m. pl.* Geloni, a people of Scythia

indignor (1) be angry, be indignant, complain, protest

indomitus, -a, -um wild, fierce, untamed

Leleges, -um, *m. pl.* Lelegians, early inhabitants of the coast of Asia Minor

mollis, -e soft, gentle

Morini, -orum, *m.* Morini, a tribe from Belgium

Mulciber, Mulciberi, *m.* epithet for Vulcan, perhaps alluding to his ability to polish and smoothe (> **mollire**) the metalwork he crafts

Nomades, -um, *m.* Nomads, a wandering tribe

pons, pontis, *m.* bridge

Rhenus, -i, *m.* Rhine river

sagittifer, -era, -erum arrow-carrying

724–26. **genus, discinctos … Afros, Lelegas, Caras, sagittiferos … Gelonos:** all acc. dir. objs. of **finxerat,** the subject of which is **Mulciber. Nomadum genus:** peoples of northern Africa, usually called Numidian in Latin. **discinctos … Afros:** the loose-fitting clothes of the Africans are a cliché thought to indicate a lack of manliness. **Mulciber:** an archaic epithet for Vulcan, probably connected to the verb **mollio, mollire,** "to soften," since this describes the way he works the metal. **Lelegas, Caras:** both are Greek acc. **sagittiferos … Gelonos:** the people of Scythia, a quasi-mythical land far to the northeast where the warriors fought with bow and arrow on horseback. **finxerat:** plpf., reminding the reader again that the narrative actually describes a static image.

726. **Euphrates:** the river is symbolic of its land and people; its image was therefore carried in the procession. **iam mollior:** i.e., gentler because its people have now been brought under control by Octavian. **undis:** abl. of respect.

727–28. **Morini, Rhenus, Dahae, Araxes:** more conquered peoples or their symbolic representatives. **extremique hominum Morini:** members of the Belgae, a Gallic tribe. **Rhenusque bicornis:** the Rhine river. Its mouth has two outlets. **indomitique Dahae:** from around the Caspian sea. These people had been unconquered until now, at least. **pontem indignatus Araxes:** the river running through ancient Armenia. It was crossed twice, but not bridged, by Antony.

729–31. After this elaborate and detailed ECPHRASIS, Vergil provides only a brief and ambiguous description of Aeneas' reaction to it.

> Talia per clipeum Volcani, dona parentis,
> 730   miratur rerumque ignarus imagine gaudet
> attollens umero famamque et fata nepotum.

---

attollo, -ere lift up, raise

clipeus, -i, *m.* (or clipeum, -i, *n.*) round
    shield

gaudeo, -ere, gavisus sum rejoice, delight,
    take pleasure in

miror (1) be amazed, marvel at

Volcanus, -i, *m.* Vulcan, god of fire

---

729. **Talia:** acc. dir. obj. of **miratur** (730). **clipeum Volcani, dona parentis:** the second noun is in apposition to the first, but each of the modifying genitives designates a different person and serves as a succinct reminder of by whom and at whose request this armor was created.

730. **rerum … ignarus:** the scenes depicted on the shield have yet to happen from Aeneas' perspective.

731. **famamque et fata nepotum:** the juxtaposition of **famam** and **fata** plays upon the etymological relationship between the two words, which are both derived from the verb **for, fari**, "to speak." The combination thus confirms a relationship between reputation and destiny. There may even be a HENDIADYS here: i.e., the reputation of his descendants' destiny.

Book 11.498–596

The Death of Camilla—Introduction

At the close of Book 7, Vergil provides a catalogue of Italian chieftains who enlist themselves and their armies in Turnus' campaign against the Trojans. Among these leaders are representatives of all the great peoples of ancient Italy, who join together against a common foe; each leader brings to the alliance some of the distinctive features that will eventually become a part of the Roman national character. The final character to be introduced in Vergil's catalogue (*Aen.* 7.803–17) is the warrior Camilla, queen of the Volscians (Latin *Volsci*), whose exceptional presence in the otherwise all-male entourage of Turnus is underlined by Vergil's placement of her description in the last and most memorable position in the list.

In his characterization of Camilla and her Volscian troops, Vergil explicitly compares them to the Amazons, a mythical tribe of warrior-women thought in antiquity to live just beyond the boundaries of the civilized world (*Aen.* 11.648–63). Yet this same comparison also implies how different Camilla is from them—she is no exotic foreigner, but a native of Italy and thus a symbolic ancestor of the Romans. In Book 11, Camilla seizes the opportunity to demonstrate on the battlefield her support for Turnus and his cause; her resulting death, like that of the young Pallas in Book 10, adds to the pathos created by Vergil for the losers.

In the first selection from Book 11 presented here, Vergil introduces a remarkable sympathy for Camilla into his narrative by giving us her "back story" (ANALEPSIS), explaining how a girl came to be a warrior-maiden. Scholars have noted several problems in the interpretation of this passage, caused for the most part by the fact that the goddess Diana, who speaks here of her love for Camilla, rather oddly uses the third person rather than the first to speak about herself. Some have thought this a sign of the incomplete state of the *Aeneid* at the time of Vergil's death; others have blamed the oddities of the passage on the oddness of the story itself. In these notes, I shall present what I believe to be the most likely approach to the passage, working as always on the assumption that we have here reasonably good access to what Vergil actually wrote, and intended to write; where exceptional features present themselves, I shall draw the reader's attention to them. Whatever textual and interpretive problems may remain in this passage, its exceptional contribution to the sympathy we feel for Aeneas' opponents is evident throughout.

498–521. Camilla and Turnus meet on the battlefield, and agree to collaborate in distracting and undermining the Trojans.

> Obvia cui Volscorum acie comitante Camilla
> occurrit portisque ab equo regina sub ipsis
> 500   desiluit, quam tota cohors imitata relictis
> ad terram defluxit equis; tum talia fatur:
> "Turne, sui merito siqua est fiducia forti,
> audeo et Aeneadum promitto occurrere turmae
> solaque Tyrrhenos equites ire obvia contra.

---

acies, aciei, *f.* a sharp edge; a line of vision; a battle line

Aeneades, -ae, *m.* companion or descendant of Aeneas, Trojan

Camilla, -ae, *f.* Camilla, queen of the Volscians

cohors, cohortis, *f.* cohort, subdivision of a legion, armed force

comitor, -ari, comitatus accompany, attend, escort

defluo, -ere, defluxi, defluxus flow down, glide down, descend

desilio, -ire, desilui jump down, dismount

eques, equitis, *m.* horseman, rider, knight; cavalry

fiducia, -ae, *f.* assurance, confidence, reliance, trust

imitor, -ari, imitatus imitate, copy, follow

merito *adv.* deservedly, justly

obvius, -a, -um meeting, so as to meet, to meet

occurro, -ere, occurri, occursus run to meet, hurry

promitto, -ere, promisi, promissus send forth, let loose; promise

turma, -ae, *f.* squadron, company

Turnus, -i, *m.* Turnus, king of the Rutulians

Tyrrhenus, -a, -um Etruscan, Tyrrhenian

Volsci, -orum, *m. pl.* Volscians, a people of Latium

---

498. **cui**: dat. with **obvia**, or with **occurrit** (499). The antecedent of the rel. pronoun is Turnus, whose race onto the battlefield has just been described. When a rel. pronoun appears at or near the beginning of a sentence, it is best translated with a personal or demonstrative pronoun, e.g., "(to) him" or "(to) that man." **acie comitante**: abl. abs.

499. **portis ... sub ipsis**: Camilla meets Turnus just outside the city gates. **regina**: Camilla's status as leader of the Volsci is emphasized.

500–501. **quam**: dir. obj. of **imitata. tota cohors**: her troops. **relictis ... equis**: abl. abs. **defluxit**: this verb usually describes the movement of water, but here suggests a METAPHOR for the gliding of the women-warriors down from their horses.

502. **sui ... fiducia**: trust in oneself; **sui** is objective gen. **siqua**: equivalent to **si** + **(ali)qua. forti**: dat. of reference or possession.

503. **Aeneadum = Aeneadarum. occurrere**: pres. inf. instead of the normal fut. inf. with **promitto. turmae**: dat. with compound verb.

504. **Tyrrhenos equites**: acc. with **contra**. The reversal of the usual word order is ANASTROPHE.

Me sine prima manu temptare pericula belli,   505
tu pedes ad muros subsiste et moenia serva."
Turnus ad haec oculos horrenda in virgine fixus:
"O decus Italiae virgo, quas dicere grates
quasve referre parem? Sed nunc, est omnia quando
iste animus supra, mecum partire laborem.   510
Aeneas, ut fama fidem missique reportant
exploratores, equitum levia improbus arma
praemisit, quaterent campos; ipse ardua montis
per deserta iugo superans adventat ad urbem.

---

advento (1) approach, draw near, arrive

decus, decoris, *n.* honor, glory

eques, equitis, *m.* horseman, rider, knight; cavalry

explorator, exploratoris, *m.* scout, spy

grates, -ium, *f. pl.* thanks, thanksgiving

horrendus, -a, -um terrible, awe inspiring, venerable

improbus, -a, -um unprincipled, shameless, presumptuous, wicked

iste, ista, istud that, that of yours

Italia, -ae, *f.* Italy

levis, -e light, light-weight

partior, -iri, partitus share, divide up

pedes, peditis, *m.* foot soldier, infantryman

periculum, -i, *n.* danger, trial

praemitto, -ere, praemisi, praemissus send ahead

quando when, since, as

quatio, -ere, —, quassus shake, disturb, cause to tremble

reporto (1) take back, report

sino, -ere, sivi, situs leave, let, allow, permit

subsisto, -ere, substiti stand firm, stay in place

supra (+*acc.*) on top of, above; (*adv.*) on top, higher

---

505. **prima:** modifies **pericula. manu:** abl. of means; "by hand" is equivalent here to "by force," i.e., with one's own hands. **temptare:** complementary inf. with **sine.**

506. **pedes:** nom. sing., in apposition to **tu.**

507. **(respondit) ad haec. oculos … fixus:** the perf. pass. participle functions like a Greek middle participle here, and takes an acc. obj. (also understandable as acc. of respect): *having fixed his eyes* (lit., *having been fixed with respect to his eyes*).

508. **decus Italiae:** Turnus' complimentary opening words are in strong contrast to the epithet **horrenda** used by Vergil in the preceding line to describe Camilla. **virgo:** in apposition to **decus.**

509–10. **parem (tibi):** deliberative subjunctive. **est omnia quando iste animus supra = quando animus iste est supra omnia.** The clause combines ANASTROPHE and HYPERBATON. **partire:** imperative of deponent verb.

511–12. **fama … missique … exploratores:** two separate subjects, constituting a HENDIADYS: *rumor and the scouts* is equivalent to *rumor of (i.e., carried back by) the scouts.*

513–14. **quaterent:** impf. subjunctive in an implied indir. command after **praemisit;** understand **ut. ardua:** neut. pl. acc. used substantively; obj. of **superans.**

515   Furta paro belli convexo in tramite silvae,
        ut bivias armato obsidam milite fauces.
        Tu Tyrrhenum equitem conlatis excipe signis;
        tecum acer Messapus erit turmaeque Latinae
        Tiburtique manus, ducis et tu concipe curam."
520   Sic ait, et paribus Messapum in proelia dictis
        hortatur sociosque duces et pergit in hostem.

---

armo (1) arm, equip, furnish

bivius, -a, -um crossable both ways, having two ways

concipio, -ere, concepi, conceptus take, undertake, assume

confero, conferre, contuli, collatus carry, direct, engage

convexus, -a, -um convex, rounded, vaulted, domed

eques, equitis, *m.* horseman, rider, knight; cavalry

excipio, -ere, excepi, exceptus take, take up

fauces, -ium, *f. pl.* throat; entrance, pass, passage

furtum, -i, *n.* theft; secret, deception; stratagem

Latinus, -a, -um Latin, belonging to Latium

Messapus, -i, *m.* Messapus, an Italian leader

miles, militis, *m.* soldier, soldiery, troops

obsido, -ere besiege, occupy, take possession of

pergo, -ere, perrexi, perrectus proceed, go on

proelium, -i, *n.* battle, conflict

Tiburtus, -i, *m.* Tiburtus, a founder of Tibur

trames, tramitis, *m.* footpath, path

turma, -ae, *f.* squadron, company

Tyrrhenus, -a, -um Etruscan, Tyrrhenian

---

515. **furta ... belli**: an ambush. **convexo in tramite silvae**: either the path runs through low-lying ground, and the overarching trees create a vault over it, or the path traces a curved route on the ground in the forest. In either case, **convexo** suggests the potential for deception in the landscape.

516. **ut ...obsidam**: purpose clause. **bivias ... fauces**: the outer element in a CHIASMUS. **armato ... milite**: abl. of means; Turnus speaks of his troops in the collective sing. as a fighting machine rather than a group of men.

517. **conlatis ... signis**: the idiom **signa conferre** means *to engage* (i.e., in battle).

518. **Messapus**: another of the Italian leaders, mentioned along with Turnus and Camilla in the catalogue of Italian leaders at the end of Book 7 (see especially 7.691–94). The epithet **acer** is particularly appropriate for him, since Vergil reports at 7.692 that Messapus could not be harmed by fire or by steel.

519. **Tiburti**: Tiburtus too was mentioned in the earlier catalogue, at 7.671.

522–31. Vergil briefly sets the scene for Turnus' withdrawal from the battlefield. Superficially, his absence is what allows Camilla to command all of our attention; it also sets the stage for the treachery and deception that will lead to Camilla's death, as Turnus retires into ambush.

> Est curvo anfractu valles, accommoda fraudi
> armorumque dolis, quam densis frondibus atrum
> urget utrimque latus, tenuis quo semita ducit
> angustaeque ferunt fauces aditusque maligni. 525
> Hanc super in speculis summoque in vertice montis
> planities ignota iacet tutique receptus,

---

accommodus, -a, -um suitable for, convenient for

aditus, -us, *m.* approach, entrance, pass

anfractus, -us, *m.* bend, winding course, spiral

angustus, -a, -um narrow, thin, confined, tight

curvus, -a, -um curved, winding, tortuous, twisting

densus, -a, -um dense, thick, close-packed

fauces, -ium, *f. pl.* throat; entrance, pass, passage

fraus, fraudis, *f.* mischief, deceit, guile

frons, frondis, *f.* foliage, leafy bough

ignotus, -a, -um unfamiliar, unknown

malignus, -a, -um ungenerous, scanty, spiteful, unkind

planities, -ei, *f.* level surface, flat space, plateau

receptus, -us, *m.* retreat, shelter, refuge

semita, -ae, *f.* path, track

specula, -ae, *f.* lookout, watch-tower, height

tenuis, -e slender, narrow, thin

tutus, -a, -um protected, safe, secure

urgeo, -ere, ursi press, urge, encroach on

utrimque *adv.* on both sides

valles, -is, *f.* valley

522–23. **Est ... valles**: the introduction to an ECPHRASIS, or detailed description of a location, natural phenomenon, or work of art. **fraudi ... dolis**: dat. with **accommoda**. **densis frondibus**: abl. of description or characteristic; construe with **atrum**.

524–25. **latus**: the steep side or flank of the hill; the two flanks create a natural (and treacherous) mountain pass. **semita, fauces, aditus**: all describe essentially the same thing, i.e., the access to the pass; implicit in the difficulty of approaching it is the even greater difficulty of escaping from it. **maligni**: emphatically completes a CHIASMUS and suggests at least a hint of

PATHETIC FALLACY.

526. **Hanc super**: ANASTROPHE, i.e., a reversal of the usual word order.

527. **ignota**: here, used in its passive sense, i.e., unfamiliar/unknown to humans. **iacet**: the sing. verb has two subjects, **planities** and **receptus**, the second of which is pl. The sing. verb is justified, however, both by its placement immediately after the sing. subject and by the collective character of both subjects; i.e., the two subjects contribute to a single unified picture of the landscape, and their close relationship is underlined by CHIASMUS.

seu dextra laevaque velis occurrere pugnae
sive instare iugis et grandia volvere saxa.
530   Huc iuvenis nota fertur regione viarum
arripuitque locum et silvis insedit iniquis.

---

arripio, -ere, arripui, arreptus snatch, seize, take possession of

grandis, -e great, large

iniquus, -a, -um uneven, unfair, rough, treacherous

insideo, -ere, insedi, insessus sit in, lie in ambush, rest upon

insto, -are, institi stand on; assail, press, urge on

notus, -a, -um known

occurro, -ere, occurri, occursus run to meet, hurry

regio, regionis, *f.* area, direction, region, line

seu, sive either. . . or; whether. . . or

528–29. velis: pres. potential subjunctive. The vividness of the ECPHRASIS is enhanced by this unusual second-person address to the reader: Vergil places his reader in the middle of the action (and the treachery) about to unfold. **occurrere, instare, volvere:** complementary infs. with **velis. pugnae:** dat. with **occurrere. iugis:** abl. of place where.

530. iuvenis: Turnus.

531. silvis ... iniquis: both literally and metaphorically: the forests are unevenly scattered over the steeply inclining hillsides, and are treacherously unfair to those who approach them unwarily.

532–96. The scene changes to Olympus, where Diana addresses one of her attendants, the nymph Opis. In her speech, Diana offers an explanation for Camilla's unique status among her favorites, and also indicates her awareness of Camilla's impending doom. Her tale of Camilla's childhood is an example of ANALEPSIS, i.e., a flashback to events occurring outside the dramatic time of the *Aeneid*. Diana closes her speech by asking Opis to help her in avenging Camilla's death.

> Velocem interea superis in sedibus Opim,
> unam ex virginibus sociis sacraque caterva,
> compellabat et has tristis Latonia voces
> ore dabat: "Graditur bellum ad crudele Camilla,   535
> o virgo, et nostris nequiquam cingitur armis,
> cara mihi ante alias. Neque enim novus iste Dianae
> venit amor subitaque animum dulcedine movit.

---

caterva, -ae, *f.* band, crowd, throng, company
compello (1) address, speak to
Diana, -ae, *f.* Diana, virgin goddess of the hunt and the moon
dulcedo, dulcedinis, *f.* sweetness, pleasantness
gradior, gradi, gressus step, walk, proceed

iste, ista, istud that, that of yours
Latonius, -a, -um of or having to do with Leto (Latona), mother of Apollo and Diana
nequiquam *adv.* in vain, uselessly
Opis (*or* **Ops**), **Opis,** *f.* Opis, a nymph
velox, velocis swift, rapid, speedy

---

532. **Opim**: Greek acc., dir. obj. of **compellabat** (534). Opis is known from Hellenistic Greek literature as a title of Diana herself; here, she is a favorite attendant of the goddess.

533. **unam ex virginibus**: partitive construction consisting of a number + **ex** + abl. indicating the larger whole. Cf. the simile at *Aen.* 1.498–504, where the entrance of Dido surrounded by a crowd of Carthaginians is compared to the entrance of Diana surrounded by a crowd of her attendants. **ex virginibus ... caterva**: CHIASMUS emphasizes the group's inseparability.

534. **tristis Latonia**: the adj. **tristis** is ominous, foreshadowing Camilla's imminent death; the epithet **Latonia** is a reminder of Diana's mother, and so casts Diana herself in a maternal role.

535–36. **crudele**: the foreshadowing continues, for the war will be cruel indeed to Camilla; the effect is continued with **nequiquam. o virgo**: Diana addresses Opis; her

use of the word **virgo** parallels Vergil's repeated use of it in this scene to refer to Camilla. **nostris ... armis**: the weapons of Diana are those used for hunting, not war; Diana's irony suggests from the outset that her speech is doomed to die in battle.

537–38. **Dianae**: if Diana is speaking here, her reference to herself in the third person seems rather strange; some editors have therefore attributed some of the following lines to Opis rather than to Diana (see my introductory note to this passage, above). Yet only Diana would know the details of Camilla's birth and upbringing, as described in the following lines, and Opis herself is little more than an intermediary in this scene. I have therefore maintained throughout the punctuation that attributes all of 535–94 to Diana. **novus iste ... amor subitaque ... dulcedine**: Diana's strong feelings for Camilla are not new, but go back to the circumstances of her birth.

Pulsus ob invidiam regno viresque superbas
540   Priverno antiqua Metabus cum excederet urbe,
infantem fugiens media inter proelia belli
sustulit exsilio comitem, matrisque vocavit
nomine Casmillae mutata parte Camillam.
Ipse sinu prae se portans iuga longa petebat
545   solorum nemorum: tela undique saeva premebant
et circumfuso volitabant milite Volsci.

Casmilla, -ae, *f.* Casmilla, mother of
    Camilla
circumfundo, -ere, circumfudi,
    circumfusus pour around, surround
excedo, -ere, excessi, excessus go away,
    depart, leave
exsilium, -i, *n.* banishment, exile
infans, infantis, *m./f.* baby, infant
invidia, -ae, *f.* ill will, envy, jealousy
Metabus, -i, *m.* Metabus, one-time ruler of
    Privernum

miles, militis, *m.* soldier, soldiery, troops
prae (+*abl.*) in front of, before
Privernum, -i, *n.* Privernum, a Latin town,
    chief town of the Volscians
proelium, -i, *n.* battle, conflict
sinus, -us, *m.* fold; bosom; embrace
volito (1) fly about, move rapidly about
Volsci, -orum, *m. pl.* Volscians, a people
    of Latium

---

539. **ob invidiam ... viresque superbas**:
HENDIADYS; i.e., the envy of his people was
directed at Metabus because of his use of
arrogant force. **regno**: abl. of separation
with **pulsus**.

540. **Priverno**: abl. in apposition with
antiqua ... urbe, abl. of separation or place
from which with **excederet**. Privernum
was the chief city of the Volscians. Its ruler
Metabus was driven out by enemies, much
as several other characters in the *Aeneid*
were driven from their homes.

541–42. **infantem**: dir. obj. of **sustulit**.
comitem: in apposition with **infantem**. Not
until 543 do we learn that this child is a girl;
the postponement of any indication of her
gender adds to the surprise and unusualness
of her situation. **exsilio**: abl. of specification
or dat. of purpose with **comitem**. **matris**:
the indirect mention of her mother implies
that she has died or otherwise disappeared,
although Vergil provides no details.

543. **Casmillae ... Camilla**: Vergil is
quite explicit about the etymology for
Camilla's name, which is probably to be
connected with a rare Latin word (*camil-
lus*) used to describe a priest's young at-
tendant—in this case, she will become an
attendant (see below, 558) of Diana. Her
mother's name, on the other hand, appears
to be connected to the Latin word for the
Muses, *Casmenae*. **nomine**: abl. of specifica-
tion with **vocavit** (542).

544. **ipse**: the emphatic pronoun redirects
our attention to the baby's father, Metabus.
sinu prae se (eam) portans: the word order
suggests his protective embrace.

546. **circumfuso ... milite**: abl. abs.; the
sing. noun is used as a collective, of a body
of soldiers acting in unison. **Volsci**: Meta-
bus is one against many; his own people
drive him out.

Ecce fugae medio summis Amasenus abundans
spumabat ripis, tantus se nubibus imber
ruperat. Ille innare parans infantis amore
tardatur caroque oneri timet. Omnia secum 550
versanti subito vix haec sententia sedit:
telum immane manu valida quod forte gerebat
bellator, solidum nodis et robore cocto,
huic natam libro et silvestri subere clausam
implicat atque habilem mediae circumligat hastae; 555

---

abundo (1) overflow, be abundant

Amasenus, -i, *m.* Amasenus, a river of southern Latium

bellator, bellatoris, *m.* fighter, warrior

circumligo (1) bind, tie, fasten

claudo, -ere, clausi, clausus close, confine, enclose, envelop

coquo, -ere, coxi, coctus harden by heat, bake, cook

forte *adv.* by chance, accidentally, fortuitously

habilis, -e easy to handle, easily fitted

hasta, -ae, *f.* spear, javelin

imber, imbris, *m.* rain, shower, rainstorm

implico (1) enfold, entwine, wrap

infans, infantis, *m./ f.* baby, infant

inno (1) swim in, swim

liber, libri, *m.* inner bark of a tree, bark

nata, -ae, *f.* daughter, young girl

nodus, -i, *m.* knot

onus, oneris, *n.* burden, load

ripa, -ae, *f.* bank (of a river)

sententia, -ae, *f.* idea, opinion, belief, decision

silvestris, -e woodland, belonging to woods

solidus, -a, -um solid, firm, strong

suber, suberis, *n.* cork-oak, cork

subito *adv.* suddenly

tardo (1) check, slow down, hold back

timeo, -ere, timui fear, be afraid, fear for

validus, -a, -um powerful, strong

verso (1) turn, revolve, turn over, ponder

547–49. **ecce:** the visual effect suggests that we see the river from Metabus' perspective as he runs. **medio:** abl. of place; adj. used substantively. **summis ... ripis:** probably abl. of place, although dat. with **abundans** is also possible. **Amasenus:** a river that runs through southern Latium. **se ... ruperat:** the obj. of this transitive verb must be expressed in Latin, even though it is unnecessary in English. **nubibus:** abl. of separation. **infantis:** objective gen. with **amore. amore:** abl. of means.

550–51. **caro ... oneri:** dat. indir. obj. with **timet,** *he is afraid on behalf of his dear burden.* **omnia:** dir. obj. of **versanti. versanti:** dat. indir. obj. with **sedit,** or dat. of reference.

552. **manu valida:** abl. of means. **quod:** acc.; its antecedent is nom. **telum.**

553. **bellator:** emphatic ENJAMBMENT. **nodis et robore cocto:** abl. of cause, specification, or description with **solidum.**

554. **huic:** refers to **telum** (552), originally introduced as a nom. but now to be construed as dat. with the verb **implicat.** This discontinuity in syntax (called ANACOLUTHON) reflects Metabus' confusion as he must decide in haste how to get his daughter safely across the river. **libro et silvestri subere:** abl. of means with **clausam;** HENDIADYS, i.e., with/in the bark of a forest cork-tree.

555. **habilem:** refers to the child, **natam** (554); because of her small size and flexible limbs she is easily handled and can therefore be fitted closely to the spearshaft. **mediae ... hastae:** dat with compound verb **circumligat.**

quam dextra ingenti librans ita ad aethera fatur:
'Alma, tibi hanc, nemorum cultrix, Latonia virgo,
ipse pater famulam voveo; tua prima per auras
tela tenens supplex hostem fugit. Accipe, testor,
560   diva tuam, quae nunc dubiis committitur auris.'
Dixit et adducto contortum hastile lacerto
immittit: sonuere undae, rapidum super amnem

---

adduco, -ere, adduxi, adductus lead to, bring to; draw to the body

almus, -a, -um nurturing, fostering, kindly

amnis, amnis, *m./f.* river

committo, -ere, commisi, commissus bring together, expose to, entrust to

contorqueo, -ere, contorsi, contortus twist, turn, agitate, send whirling, discharge

cultrix, cultricis, *f.* female inhabitant, dweller

dubius, -a, -um uncertain, doubtful, unreliable

famula, -ae, *f.* serving woman, maid, attendant

hastile, hastilis, *n.* spear, handle of a spear

immitto, -ere, immisi, immissus send, throw

ita *adv.* thus, in this way

lacertus, -i, *m.* and **lacertum, -i,** *n.* arm, upper arm

Latonius, -a, -um of or having to do with Leto (Latona), mother of Apollo and Diana

libro (1) level, balance, aim

rapidus, -a, -um swift, rapid

testor, testari, testatus call to witness, appeal to

---

556. **quam**: i.e., **hanc hastam**.

557. **alma**: the epithet acts as a sort of suggestion—Metabus hopes that Diana will indeed be kind to his child. **nemorum cultrix**: one of the standard attributes of Diana. **Latonia**: another reminder that Diana herself is the daughter of someone whose children were threatened.

558–59. **famulam**: typically a female divinity has female attendants to oversee her rituals and other needs. **tua ... tela**: Metabus reminds Diana that the spear is the weapon most closely associated with her; the spear to which he ties his daughter is therefore already Diana's. **prima**: modifies the implied subject of **fugit**, Camilla. From her earliest moments, she has devoted herself to Diana. **supplex**: because she is dependent upon the goddess for her survival.

560. **diva tuam**: the juxtaposition symbolizes the close relationship desired by Metabus between goddess and girl. **dubiis ... auris**: doubtful from his perspective, i.e., not to be relied upon except out of extraordinary necessity.

561. **adducto ... lacerto**: Metabus pulls back his arm in preparation for throwing the spear. **contortum**: in the process, the spear itself is twisted.

562. **sonuere**: alternate third pers. pl. perf. **undae**: poetic equivalent of **aquae**.

infelix fugit in iaculo stridente Camilla.
At Metabus magna propius iam urgente caterva
dat sese fluvio, atque hastam cum virgine victor 565
gramineo, donum Triviae, de caespite vellit.
Non illum tectis ullae, non moenibus urbes
accepere (neque ipse manus feritate dedisset),
pastorum et solis exegit montibus aevum.
Hic natam in dumis interque horrentia lustra 570

---

aevum, -i, *n.* age, span of time, lifetime

caespes, caespitis, *m.* sod, turf, ground

caterva, -ae, *f.* band, crowd, throng, company

dumus, -i, *m.* briar, thornbush

exigo, -ere, exegi, exactus drive out; extend, undergo, spend (time)

feritas, feritatis, *f.* savagery, fierceness, ferocity

fluvius, -i, *m.* river, stream

gramineus, -a, -um grassy

hasta, -ae, *f.* spear, javelin

iaculum, -i, *n.* javelin

lustra, -orum, *n. pl.* wilds, lairs

Metabus, -i, *m.* Metabus, one-time ruler of Privernum

nata, -ae, *f.* daughter, young girl

pastor, pastoris, *m.* shepherd

propius *adv.* nearer, more closely

strideo, -ere and strido, -ere, stridi hiss, whirr, whistle, make a high-pitched sound

Trivia, -ae, *f.* Trivia, another name for Diana

urgeo, -ere, ursi press, urge, encroach on

vello, -ere, velli, vulsus pull out, pull up, extract

---

563. **infelix**: the adj. is striking here—why is Camilla called "unlucky" by Diana as she describes how Metabus attempted to save her? Presumably Diana is thinking primarily of Camilla's misfortune to be deprived of her homeland simply because she is Metabus' daughter; but the epithet also foreshadows the conclusion of Camilla's *aristeia*. Diana may also be using the adj. in its most literal sense, "infertile," "not productive (of offspring)"—because Metabus has just promised the girl to Diana; since Diana's attendants, like Diana herself, are perpetual virgins, Camilla is now destined to have no children.

565. **fluvio**: dat. indir. obj. **cum virgine**: abl. of accompaniment. **victor**: in apposition to the implied subject, Metabus.

566. **donum**: acc. in apposition to **hastam cum virgine**—both the spear and the child

tied to it are dedicated to Diana. **Triviae**: an epithet for Diana, goddess of the crossroads; again Diana refers to herself in the third person.

567–68. **non illum tectis ullae, non moenibus urbes/ accepere**: the combination of ANAPHORA, ASYNDETON, and SYNCHYSIS allows Vergil to use only once words that we would use twice in English to express the same idea: *no cities received him* in their dwellings, *no cities received him* in their walls. **feritate**: abl. of cause. **dedisset**: plpf. subjunctive in the apodosis of a past contrary-to-fact condition; the protasis is unexpressed.

570. **natam**: acc. dir. obj. of **nutribat** (572). **horrentia lustra**: bristling both from the wild overgrowth and the shaggy wild animals.

armentalis equae mammis et lacte ferino
nutribat teneris immulgens ubera labris.
Utque pedum primis infans vestigia plantis
institerat, iaculo palmas armavit acuto
575   spiculaque ex umero parvae suspendit et arcum.
Pro crinali auro, pro longae tegmine pallae
tigridis exuviae per dorsum a vertice pendent.
Tela manu iam tum tenera puerilia torsit

---

acutus, -a, -um pointed, sharp

arcus, -us, *m.* bow

armentalis, -e having to do with herds, rustic

armo (1) arm, equip, furnish

crinalis, -e worn in the hair

dorsum, -i, *n.* back

equa, -ae, *f.* mare

exuviae, -arum, *f. pl.* armor, spoils; skin stripped from dead beast

ferinus, -a, -um wild, belonging to wild beasts

iaculum, -i, *n.* javelin

immulgeo, -ere milk

infans, infantis, *m./f.* baby, infant

labrum, -i, *n.* lip

lac, lactis, *n.* milk

mamma, -ae, *f.* teat, udder

nutrio, -ire, nutrivi, nutritus nourish, feed

palla, -ae, *f.* cloak, mantle, garment

palma, -ae, *f.* palm, hand

parvus, -a, -um small, little

pendeo, -ere, pependi (intrans.) or pendo, -ere, pependi, pensus (trans.) hang

planta, -ae, *f.* sole (of the foot); treading, walking, step

puerilis, -e of a child, belonging to a child

spiculum, -i, *n.* point of a weapon, arrow

suspendo, -ere, suspendi, suspensus hang, hang up

tegmen, tegminis, *n.* covering

tener, tenera, tenerum tender, delicate, of tender age

tigris, tigridis, *f.* tiger

uber, uberis, *n.* teat, udder

---

571. **mammis et lacte ferino**: abl. of means; HENDIADYS.

572. **nutribat**: an archaic spelling for the regular **nutriebat**; this archaic form is appropriate in a narrative about an earlier and simpler time. **teneris ... labris**: dat. of direction with **immulgens**—he is milking the horse's teats into his daughter's mouth.

574. **iaculo ... acuto**: abl. of means.

575. **spiculaque ... et arcum**: the massive hunting gear literally surrounds the small child (**parvae**).

576. **crinali auro**: ornamentation of the hair that would normally be worn by the daughter of a Roman aristocrat. **pallae**: the long cloak, falling to the feet, worn as an overgarment by Roman women. The

clothing described here would not only be incongruous for Camilla, but is also anachronistic. The description is marked by a combination of ANAPHORA and ASYNDETON.

577. **tigridis**: the contrast between the domesticated female whose appearance is evoked in the previous line and the wildness of Camilla is suggested by the animal-skin she wears. **exuviae**: perhaps taken by Metabus in an earlier hunt. **a vertice**: Camilla's head is covered by the head of the tiger, worn as a sort of helmet.

578. **tela ... puerilia**: ironic, since normally the playthings of a child are toys. **manu iam tum tenera**: the adverbs are an ironic reminder of how young she is.

et fundam tereti circum caput egit habena
Strymoniamque gruem aut album deiecit olorem.   580
Multae illam frustra Tyrrhena per oppida matres
optavere nurum; sola contenta Diana
aeternum telorum et virginitatis amorem
intemerata colit. Vellem haud correpta fuisset
militia tali conata lacessere Teucros: 585
cara mihi comitumque foret nunc una mearum.
Verum age, quandoquidem fatis urgetur acerbis,

---

acerbus, -a, -um bitter, hostile, cruel

aeternus, -a, -um eternal, everlasting

albus, -a, -um white

conor, -ari, conatus try, attempt

contentus, -a, -um content, satisfied, happy

corripio, -ere, corripui, correptus snatch, seize, take hold of

deicio, -ere, deieci, deiectus cause to fall, strike, shoot down

Diana, -ae, *f.* Diana, virgin goddess of the hunt and the moon

frustra *adv.* in vain, uselessly

funda, -ae, *f.* sling (for hurling stones)

grus, gruis, *f.* crane, large bird

habena, -ae, *f.* rein, strap, cord

intemeratus, -a, -um undefiled, pure, inviolate

lacesso, -ere, lacessivi (or **-ii**)**, lacessitus** challenge, provoke, arouse

militia, -ae, *f.* military service

nurus, -us, *f.* daughter-in-law

olor, oloris, *m.* swan

oppidum, -i, *n.* town

quandoquidem since, seeing that

Strymonius, -a, -um belonging to the river Strymon, Strymonian

teres, teretis smooth

Tyrrhenus, -a, -um Etruscan, Tyrrhenian

urgeo, -ere, ursi press, urge, encroach on

verum *adv.* but

virginitas, virginitatis, *f.* virginity

---

580. **Strymoniamque gruem**: the crane is typically associated with the river Strymon, located in the wilds of Thrace (to the northeast of the Greek mainland). The epithet can be compared to that in the phrase "Canadian geese."

581. **multae ... matres**: i.e., the married women of the Etruscan cities, many of whom had sons for whom they sought worthy wives.

582. **optavere**: alternate third person pl. perf. **nurum**: in apposition to **illam** (581). **sola ... Diana**: abl. of cause with **contenta**.

583. The unusual four-word hexameter (with **et** being considered a proclitic, not a discrete word) is marked by CHIASMUS.

584–85. **vellem**: impf. subjunctive, used to express a past potential. **haud = non.** **correpta fuisset**: plpf. subjunctive in a contrary-to-fact wish; after **vellem**, no subordinating conjunction (e.g., **ut** or **si**) is required. **militia tali**: abl. of means.

586. **cara mihi**: cf. the same phrase at the beginning of Diana's speech (537). **foret = esset.** The impf. subjunctive is used to express the unfulfilled consequence of her contrary-to-fact wish, in a construction analogous to the apodosis in a condition.

587. **verum age**: Diana abruptly changes her tone, as she shifts from speaking about what could have been to the situation as it in fact stands. **fatis urgetur acerbis**: Diana implicitly acknowledges her helplessness to avert the power of fate.

labere, nympha, polo finesque invise Latinos,
tristis ubi infausto committitur omine pugna.

590   Haec cape et ultricem pharetra deprome sagittam:
Hac, quicumque sacrum violarit vulnere corpus,
Tros Italusque, mihi pariter det sanguine poenas.
Post ego nube cava miserandae corpus et arma
inspoliata feram tumulo patriaeque reponam."

595   Dixit, at illa levis caeli delapsa per auras
insonuit nigro circumdata turbine corpus.

---

circumdo, -are, circumdedi, circumdatus
place around, surround, enclose

committo, -ere, commisi, commissus
bring together, expose to, entrust to

delabor, delabi, delapsus descend, glide
down

depromo, -ere, deprompsi, depromptus
fetch, take out, extract

dubius, -a, -um uncertain, doubtful,
unreliable

infaustus, -a, -um ill-starred, unlucky,
cursed

insono, -are, insonui make a sound,
resound

inspoliatus, -a, -um not plundered, not
despoiled

inviso, -ere, invisi, invisus go to see, visit

Italus, -a, -um Italian

Latinus, -a, -um Latin

levis, -e light, light-weight

miserandus, -a, -um pitiable, poor

niger, nigra, nigrum black, dark

nympha, -ae, *f.* nymph

pariter *adv.* equally, evenly, likewise

pharetra, -ae, *f.* quiver

polus, -i, *m.* sky, heaven

sagitta, -ae, *f.* arrow

Tros, Trois, *m.* Tros, a Trojan [grandson of
Dardanus]

turbo, turbinis, *m.* whirlwind

ultrix, ultricis, *f.* avenger, avenging

violo (1) violate, defile

---

588. **labere:** imperative of a third-conjugation deponent verb. **polo:** abl. of separation.

589. A virtual GOLDEN LINE, ironically describing a dire scene of death and doom on earth.

590. **haec:** i.e., the quiver filled with arrows. **pharetra:** abl. of separation.

591. **hac (sagitta). violarit:** syncopated form of the fut. perf. = **violaverit.**

592. **Tros Italusque: -que** is equivalent to -ve here. **pariter:** i.e., the ethnicity of Camilla's killer will have no effect on Diana's determination to have him pay the penalty.

593. **post:** adverbial. **nube cava:** abl. of place.

594. **inspoliata:** in number and gender modifies **arma**, but should be extended to include **corpus** as well. **tumulo:** dat. of direction. **patriae:** dat. with compound verb.

595. **dixit:** Diana is the speaker. **illa:** marks the shift in subject from Diana to Opis. **levis:** nom., modifying **illa.**

596. **insonuit:** i.e., her clothing and warrior's equipment rustled as she moved. **circumdata:** perf. pass. participle used as a Greek middle—**corpus** is its obj., and **nigro turbine** is abl. of means. **corpus:** i.e., her own body.

Book 11.664–835

Between the previous excerpt (11.498–596) and this one, Vergil steps back briefly from the story of Camilla and focuses broadly on the tides of war, using a SIMILE depicting the continual backwards-and-forwards movement of the sea's waves to characterize the vicissitudes of combat as experienced by both the Trojans (with their allies) and the Italians led by Turnus. Camilla and her Volscian troops, all women, are an important part, but only part, of the chaos on the battlefield. Vergil thus both moderates, if only briefly, the high emotion of his earlier focus on Camilla, and increases in his reader a sense of foreboding surrounding the maiden's fate. In the following excerpt, Camilla returns to center stage, thus initiating the second (and final) "act" in Vergil's narrative concerning the Italian Amazon.

664–89. Camilla's *aristeia* (display of glory on the battlefield) receives elaborate and graphic description, as she turns her weapons against the Trojans and their allies.

Quem telo primum, quem postremum, aspera virgo,
deicis? Aut quot humi morientia corpora fundis?   665

---

deicio, -ere, deieci, deiectus throw down, cause to fall, strike, shoot down
humus, -i, *f.* ground, earth, soil

postremus, -a, -um last, final
quot how many?; as many as

664–65. **Quem ...deicis? aut ... fundis?**: the poet's second-person address to Camilla is unusual and therefore all the more striking. Such examples of APOSTROPHE, going back to Homer, tend to be highly emotional, and more often than not mark the character thus addressed as one whose fate is soon to be sealed. The poet thus reveals that his sympathy extends to the enemies of Aeneas and his men. **Quem ... primum, quem postremum**: the two adjs. are in apposition with **quem**. The combination of ANAPHORA, ASYNDETON, and two antonyms is emphatic. **aspera virgo**: voc. **Quem ... quem ... aut quot ... morientia corpora**: acc. dir. objs. of the two verbs **deicis** and **fundis**. The first two suggest a focus on individuals, but with the last acc. Vergil suggests that the devastation left in Camilla's wake is vast. Her accomplishments are notable for both the distinction of the individual warriors she defeats and for the number of troops she brings down. **humi**: locative.

Eunaeum Clytio primum patre, cuius apertum
adversi longa transverberat abiete pectus.
sanguinis ille vomens rivos cadit atque cruentam
mandit humum moriensque suo se in vulnere versat.
670　Tum Lirim Pagasumque super, quorum alter habenas
suffuso revolutus equo dum colligit, alter
dum subit ac dextram labenti tendit inermem,

---

abies, abietis, *f.* fir, object made of fir

adversus, -a, -um turned towards, facing, opposite

Clytius, -i, *m.* Clytius, an ally of Aeneas

colligo, -ere, collegi, collectus pick up, gather, collect

cruentus, -a, -um bloody, bleeding, stained with blood

Eunaeus, -i, *m.* Eunaeus, an ally of Aeneas

habena, -ae, *f.* rein, strap, cord

humus, -i, *f.* ground, earth, soil

inermis, -e unarmed

Liris, Liris, *m.* Liris, an ally of Aeneas

mando, -ere, mandi, mansus chew, bite, crush with teeth

Pagasus, -i, *m.* Pagasus, an ally of Aeneas

revolvo, -ere, revolvi, revolutus roll back, wind up, turn over

rivus, -i, *m.* stream, brook

suffundo, -ere, suffudi, suffusus pour on; spread beneath, stretch beneath

transverbero (1) transfix, pierce through

verso (1) turn, turn over, keep turning over, revolve, ponder

vomo, -ere, vomui, vomitus spew forth, vomit, discharge

666–67. **Eunaeum**: acc. dir. obj. of an implied verb answering the question posed in the apostrophe to Camilla (e.g., **deicit** or **fundit**). Both Eunaeus (mentioned only here in the *Aeneid*) and his father Clytius are Trojans. **Clytio ... patre**: either abl. of origin or abl. abs. **primum**: echoes **primum** in 664. **cuius**: Eunaeus is the antecedent. **apertum ... pectus**: acc. dir. obj. of **transverberat**. **adversi**: agrees with **cuius**: Camilla pierces his breast with her spear as he faces her. **longa ... abiete**: i.e., a javelin or spear made of fir; the use of the name of the material to describe the object itself is SYNECDOCHE. **abiete**: when this word is used in any case other than the nom. in Latin hexameter poetry, the -i- is consonantal, and so lengthens the preceding syllable; pronounce "AB-yeh-teh."

668–69. **sanguinis ... cruentam**: the references to blood in the first and last words in the line anticipate the bloodiness of the scene as a whole. **cruentam mandit humum**: the expression goes back to Homer's *Iliad*; see also 10.489. The blood on the ground is presumably Eunaeus' own. **suo ... in vulnere**: even as he dies, Eunaeus appears to wish to conceal the shame of a

wound inflicted by a woman. Note the elision of two monosyllables, **se + in**.

670–72. **Lirim Pagasumque**: the names of Camilla's next two victims, likewise acc. dir. objs. of an implied verb. The first is a Greek acc. **super**: adverbial, i.e., "in addition." **quorum**: Liris and Pagasus are the antecedents, here designated by **alter ... alter**. Understand an implied verb, e.g., **cadit**, with each instance of **alter**. **alter habenas suffuso revolutus equo dum colligit**: SYNCHYSIS and the postponement of **dum** reflect the chaos of the scene; read **alter revolutus dum habenas colligit suffuso equo. suffuso**: some manuscripts read **suffosso** instead. Both options make good sense: the horse falls and throws its rider either because it has sustained a wound in its belly, or because the ligaments of its knees have been cut. **dextram ... inermem**: the second friend comes to the aid of the first, and puts down his weapon to aid the dying man; this leaves his hand empty of weapons, and makes him unable to defend himself. Presumably, however, the fatal blow inflicted by Camilla is more that a superficial wound to the hand.

praecipites pariterque ruunt. His addit Amastrum
Hippotaden, sequiturque incumbens eminus hasta
Tereaque Harpalycumque et Demophoonta Chromimque;   675
quotque emissa manu contorsit spicula virgo,
tot Phrygii cecidere viri. Procul Ornytus armis
ignotis et equo venator Iapyge fertur,

Amastrus, -i, *m.* Amastrus, an ally of
  Aeneas

Chromis, -is, *m.* Chromis, an ally of
  Aeneas

contorqueo, -ere, contorsi, contortus twist,
  turn, agitate, send whirling, discharge

Demophoon, -ntis, *m.* Demophoon, an ally
  of Aeneas

eminus *adv.* from a distance, from afar

emitto, -ere, emisi, emissus send out, let
  loose, let fly, shoot

Harpalycus, -i, *m.* Harpalycus, an ally of
  Aeneas

hasta, -ae, *f.* spear, javelin

Hippotades, -ae, *m.* descendant/son of
  Hippotes

Iapyx, Iapygis Iapygian, from or
  belonging to southern Italy

ignotus, -a, -um unfamiliar, unknown

incumbo, -ere, incubui lean forward;
  apply oneself with energy

Ornytus, -i, *m.* Ornytus, an ally of Aeneas

pariter *adv.* equally, evenly, likewise,
  together

Phrygius, -a, -um Phrygian, Trojan

quot how many?; as many as

spiculum, -i, *n.* point of a weapon, arrow

Tereus, -ei *or* **-eos,** *m.* Tereus, an ally of
  Aeneas

venator, venatoris, *m.* hunter

---

673. **praecipites**: nom. in apposition with
the implied subjects of **ruunt**, Liris and
Pagasus. **pariter**: they die as they lived and
fought, as companions. **His**: dat. with **ad-
dit**. **addit**: Camilla is the subject.

674. **Hippotaden**: a Greek patronymic
with a Greek acc. ending. **sequitur**: has both
its literal sense here ("she pursues") and a
metaphorical one, as she adds to the list of
her victims. **incumbens eminus**: almost
an OXYMORON, capturing the swiftness with
which Camilla moves in on her prey: no
sooner does she spot them from afar than she
pounces upon them. **hasta**: abl. of means.

675. **Tereaque Harpalycumque et De-
mophoonta Chromimque**: Homeric-style
line, composed entirely of four names. The
accumulation of four names in a single line,
linked by POLYSYNDETON, suggests the speed
with which she dispatches her enemies; Ver-
gil implies that she kills so many so quickly
that she leaves him little opportunity for
detailed description. The names are all
Greek acc.; these characters are mentioned

only here in the *Aeneid*. The final syllable of
Demophoonta is short, since it is followed
by the combination of mute (**Ch-**) and liquid
(**-r-**) consonants. This combination allows a
preceding vowel to be construed as either
long or short, depending on the metrical re-
quirements of the line.

676. **quot**: modifies **spicula**. **emissa ...
contorsit**: a slight HYSTERON PROTERON, since
the arrows are shot forth after she takes
them in her hand and pulls it back in a
curve preparing to shoot; because of the
twisting of her hand in the process, the ar-
rows spin as they fly through the air. **manu**:
abl. of means or separation; construe with
emissa, or **contorsit**, or both.

677–78. **tot**: modifies **viri**. **cecidere**: alter-
nate third person pl. perf. **armis ignotis**:
abl. of description. **equo ... Iapyge**: like-
wise an abl. of description, but also with
specific reference to the place—in this case,
a horse—on which he is seated. **venator**: in
apposition with Ornytus. **Iapyge**: Apulian,
i.e., from southern Italy.

cui pellis latos umeros erepta iuvenco
680   pugnatori operit, caput ingens oris hiatus
et malae texere lupi cum dentibus albis,
agrestisque manus armat sparus; ipse catervis
vertitur in mediis et toto vertice supra est.
Hunc illa exceptum (neque enim labor agmine verso)
685   traicit et super haec inimico pectore fatur:
"Silvis te, Tyrrhene, feras agitare putasti?

---

agito (1) stir up, set in motion, harass

agrestis, -e rustic, of the countryside, rural

albus, -a, -um white

armo (1) arm, equip, furnish

caterva, -ae, *f.* band, crowd, throng, company, troops

dens, dentis, *m.* tooth

excipio, -ere, excepi, exceptus take, take up

fera, -ae, *f.* wild beast

hiatus, -us, *m.* opening, yawning, gaping

inimicus, -a, -um hostile, unfriendly

iuvencus, -i, *m.* calf, young ox

lupus, -i, *m.* wolf

mala, -ae, *f.* jaw(s)

operio, -ire, operui, opertus close, cover, shroud

pellis, -is, *f.* skin, hide

pugnator, pugnatoris, *m.* fighter, warrior

puto (1) think, suppose

sparus, -i, *m.* hunting spear

supra (+*acc.*) on top of, above; (*adv.*) on top, higher

tego, -ere, texi, tectus cover

traicio, -ere, traieci, traiectus throw across, pierce, transfix

Tyrrhenus, -a, -um Etruscan, Tyrrhenian

679–81. **cui:** dat. of reference looking back to **Ornytus** (677), effectively a dat. of possession here with **latos umeros. pellis:** nom. **iuvenco:** dat. of separation. **pugnatori:** probably to be construed with **cui,** although some editors take it in apposition to **iuvenco. caput:** acc. dir. obj. of **texere;** understand a second implied **cui,** as another dat. of reference/possession. **ingens oris hiatus:** the unusual mode of expression (nom. noun modified by gen. noun, as opposed to nom. noun modified by adj. or participle) places emphasis on the gaping opening for the mouth in the wolfskin covering Ornytus' head, rather than the mouth itself. **ingens ...hiatus et malae ... lupi cum dentibus albis:** Ornytus wears the wolfskin so that the animal's head is centered over his own; it thus serves as a sort of helmet as well as a visual warning to

opponents that he is as fierce as a wolf. Cf. the tiger skin worn in place of helmet and armor by Camilla, 11.577. **malae:** be careful not to confuse this noun with a form of the more common adj. **malus.**

682–83. **sparus:** a javelin for hunting. **ipse ... supra est:** his imposing stature indicates that he is a leader among his men. **toto vertice:** abl. of degree of difference.

684–85. **labor (est). agmine verso:** abl. abs. **super:** adverbial here; Ornytus has fallen, and Camilla stands over him as she speaks. **inimico pectore:** abl. of description, characterizing Camilla.

686. **silvis:** abl. of place. **te ... feras agitare:** indir. statement. **Tyrrhene:** Camilla addresses him not by his own name but by a designation of his ethnicity. **putasti:** syncopated form of the second pers. perf.

Advenit qui vestra dies muliebribus armis
verba redargueret. Nomen tamen haud leve patrum
manibus hoc referes, telo cecidisse Camillae."

---

advenio, -ire, adveni, adventus arrive at,
   come to
levis, -e light, light-weight, trivial
manes, -ium, *m.* (souls of) the dead, Hades

muliebris, -e of or belonging to a woman,
   womanly, feminine, effeminate
redarguo, -ere, redargui prove untrue,
   refute, disprove
verbum, -i, *n.* word, utterance

---

687. **advenit**: third pers. perf. indicative; note the long -e-. Its subject is **dies**. **qui**: the grammatical antecedent is **dies**, but Camilla postpones this subject until the subordinate clause. **vestra**: neut. acc. pl., modifying **verba** in the next line. **muliebribus armis**: abl. of means.

688–89. **redargueret**: impf. subjunctive in a rel. clause of characteristic (*the sort of day which could disprove*). **nomen**: Camilla's meaning is ambiguous—at first she suggests that she is speaking of Ornytus' own reputation, but by placing her own name in an emphatic position at the end of the speech (and so speaking of herself in the third person) she also implies that it is her name that he will report to the dead ancestors. **haud leve**: LITOTES. **patrum manibus**: i.e., Ornytus' dead ancestors. **referes**: fut. indicative, but with imperative force. **telo**: abl. of means. **cecidisse**: pf. inf. in indir. statement, introduced by **referes**; understand **te** as the subject (*you will bring to the underworld this reputation, i.e., that you fell*, etc.).

690–724. Camilla's *aristeia* continues. Vergil continues to maintain his narrow focus on Camilla and her individual opponents; the details of their confrontations are graphic and bloody, as Camilla repeatedly overcomes her enemies.

690   Protinus Orsilochum et Buten, duo maxima Teucrum
           corpora, sed Buten aversum cuspide fixit
           loricam galeamque inter, qua colla sedentis
           lucent et laevo dependet parma lacerto;
           Orsilochum fugiens magnumque agitata per orbem
695   eludit gyro interior sequiturque sequentem;

---

aversus, -a, -um reversed, turned away
from

Butes, -is, *m.* Butes, an ally of Aeneas

collum, -i, *n.* neck

cuspis, cuspidis, *f.* sharp point, spear,
lance

dependeo, -ere, dependi hang down

duo, duae, duo two

eludo, -ere, elusi, elusus trick, deceive,
escape, evade

galea, -ae, *f.* helmet

gyrus, -i, *m.* circle, circling movement, ring

interior, interius inner, internal, inside of

lacertus, -i, *m.* and **lacertum, -i,** *n.* arm,
upper arm

laevus, -a, -um left, left-handed

lorica, -ae, *f.* breastplate

luceo, -ere, luxi shine, gleam, glitter

Orsilochus, -i, *m.* Orsilochus, an ally of
Aeneas

parma, -ae, *f.* shield

protinus *adv.* straightaway, immediately

690–91. Buten: Greek acc. Together with **Orsilochum**, this is the dir. obj. of an implied verb, e.g., **addit** or **petit. duo maxima ... corpora:** acc., in apposition with **Orsilochum et Buten;** the expression, a SYNECDOCHE, emphasizes their sheer physical mass. **cuspide:** abl. of means.

692. loricam galeamque inter: the postponement of the prep. (ANASTROPHE) suggests the speed with which Camilla works—only after the spear has come to a stop is its position clear. **qua:** abl. of place. **colla:** nom. pl.; the pl. is a poetic convention here, when the neck of an individual is described. **sedentis:** i.e., of Butes sitting on his horse.

693. lucent: amid the the bloody armor and weapons on the battlefield, the white skin of Butes' neck gleams incongruously. **laevo ... lacerto:** abl. of separation with **dependet.**

694. Orsilochum: the abrupt transition from Butes to Orsilochus suggests that Camilla wastes little time relishing her victory.

695. eludit gyro interior: Camilla's stratagem is highly risky for her, but even more confusing for her opponent: rather than running away, she pulls inside the circle around which Orsilochus is riding, and so makes it difficult for him to face her directly.

tum validam perque arma viro perque ossa securim
altior exsurgens oranti et multa precanti
congeminat; vulnus calido rigat ora cerebro.
Incidit huic subitoque aspectu territus haesit
Appenninicolae bellator filius Auni,   700
haud Ligurum extremus, dum fallere fata sinebant.

Appenninicola, -ae, *m.* one who lives in
the Appennines, Appennine-dweller

aspectus, -us, *m.* sight, glance, vision,
view, gaze

Aunus, -i, *m.* Aunus, a man from the
mountains of northern Italy

bellator, bellatoris, *m.* fighter, warrior

calidus, -a, -um hot, warm, feverish

cerebrum, -i, *n.* brain, head, skull

congemino (1) double; use repeatedly,
strike repeatedly

exsurgo, -ere, exsurrexi rise up, stand up

filius, -i, *m.* son

incido, -ere, incidi, incasus fall upon,
chance to meet, come across

Ligus, -uris, *m.* a Ligurian, an inhabitant
of Cisalpine Gaul

os, ossis, *n.* bone

rigo (1) make wet, soak, drench

securis, -is, *f.* ax, hatchet

sino, -ere, sivi, situs leave, let, allow, permit

subitus, -a, -um sudden, unexpected

terreo, -ere, terrui, territus fill with fear,
terrify, alarm

validus, -a, -um powerful, strong

---

696. **validam ... securim**: the enclosing
word order of the noun and its adj., to-
gether with the postponement of the verb,
leaves Camilla's axe looming, so to speak,
over Orsilochus for a moment before it
comes crashing down. **perque ... perque**:
this ONOMATOPOETIC ANAPHORA anticipates
the repeated falling of Camilla's axe, and
the sound thus produced. **perque arma
viro**: this echo of the first line of the *Ae-
neid* may be thought to suggest a parallel
between the accomplishments of Camilla
and Aeneas, at least temporarily. **viro**: dat.
of reference, referring to Orsilochus; treat
as a dat. of possession.

697. **altior exsurgens**: the adjs. describe
Camilla; the combination of two adjs. with-
out a connective (ASYNDETON) is unusual
and emphatic. **oranti et ... precanti**: take
with **viro** in the preceding line. **multa**:
neut. pl. acc. obj. of **precanti**.

698. **congeminat**: the violence of Camil-
la's assault is emphasized by the ENJAMB-
MENT of the verb. **calido ... cerebro**: abl. of
means, combined with an effective use of
ALLITERATION.

699. **subito aspectu**: abl. of means with
territus.

700. **Appenninicolae**: this unusual com-
pound epithet fills the first two and a half
feet of the line, and creates an uncommon,
and CHIASTIC, four-word hexameter. It de-
scribes Aunus, the father of the otherwise
unidentified Ligurian warrior who now
faces Camilla. The Ligurians, a tribe living
in the remote northwest mountains of Italy,
were known for their fierceness and their
deceptiveness; it is striking, therefore, that
this man is so surprised and terrified by
Camilla. At Book 10.185–97, Vergil includes
the Ligurians among those who, because of
an earlier alliance with Evander, now come
to the support of the Trojans.

701. **haud ... extremus**: LITOTES; the un-
derstatement suggests that the son of Au-
nus is a man to be reckoned with. **fallere**:
understand **eum** as the subject of the inf.;
this line prepares us both for the Ligurian's
attempt at deception and for its eventual
failure.

Isque ubi se nullo iam cursu evadere pugnae
posse neque instantem reginam avertere cernit,
consilio versare dolos ingressus et astu
705   incipit haec: "Quid tam egregium, si femina forti
fidis equo? Dimitte fugam et te comminus aequo
mecum crede solo pugnaeque accinge pedestri:
iam nosces ventosa ferat cui gloria fraudem."
Dixit, at illa furens acrique accensa dolore

---

accendo, -ere, accendi, accensus enflame,
kindle, light

accingo, -ere, accinxi, accinctus gird
oneself, prepare

aequus, -a, -um level, smooth, flat

astus, -us, *m.* cunning, craft, guile

cerno, -ere, crevi, cretus distinguish,
determine, perceive

comminus *adv.* at close quarters, hand-to-
hand

consilium, -i, *n.* plan, advice, decision,
intention

dimitto, -ere, dimisi, dimissus send away,
dismiss, put away

egregius, -a, -um outstanding, pre-
eminent, excellent

evado, -ere, evasi, evasus escape, evade,
go out of

femina, -ae, *f.* woman

fido, -ere, —, fisus trust, have confidence
in, rely on

fraus, fraudis, *f.* harm, danger; deceit

gloria, -ae, *f.* glory

ingredior, ingredi, ingressus enter upon,
go into, start

insto, -are, institi stand on; assail, press,
urge on

pedester, pedestris, pedestre pedestrian,
on foot

solum, -i, *n.* soil, earth, floor

ventosus, -a, -um windy; lacking
substance; changeable; vain

verso (1) turn, turn over, keep turning
over, revolve, ponder

702–3. **se ... posse**: indir. statement after
cernit; evadere ... neque ... avertere: com-
plementary infs. with **posse. nullo ... cursu**:
abl. of means. **pugnae**: dat. of separation.

704. **consilio ... et astu**: abl. of means or
description. **versare**: complementary inf.
with **ingressus.**

705–7. **Quid tam egregium (est). femina**:
in apposition with **tu**, the implied subject of
fidis. Note the unusual elision of **tam** with
the first syllable of the following word.
forti ... equo: dat. with **fidis. te ... crede
solo**: i.e., dismount from your horse and
demonstrate confidence in your ability to
fight with me here on the battlefield itself.
solo: dat. of direction with **crede. pugnae
... pedestri**: dat. of purpose.

708. **ventosa ... gloria**: i.e., glory that is
as fickle as the breezes that spread it; sub-
ject of the indir. question introduced by
nosces ... cui. nosces: the fut. is often used
in Vergil's speeches to communicate a kind
of threat to the listener. The verb in the
indir. question, **ferat**, is pres. subjunctive.
fraudem: with his final word, the Ligurian
hints not only at the fickleness of success
but also at his own cunning and the harm
it will bring.

709. **at illa**: a strong contrast is suggested:
while the Ligurian talks, Camilla acts. **acri
... dolore**: abl. of means with **accensa.**

tradit equum comiti paribusque resistit in armis 710
ense pedes nudo puraque interrita parma.
At iuvenis vicisse dolo ratus avolat ipse
(haud mora), conversisque fugax aufertur habenis
quadripedemque citum ferrata calce fatigat.
"Vane Ligus frustraque animis elate superbis, 715
nequiquam patrias temptasti lubricus artes,

---

avolo (1) fly away, fly off

calx, calcis, *f.* heel

citus, -a, -um swift, speedy

converto, -ere, converti, conversus rotate, reverse, turn backwards

effero, efferre, extuli, elatus carry away, lift

fatigo (1) tire out, exhaust; assail, harass

ferratus, -a, -um iron covered, armored

frustra *adv.* in vain, uselessly

fugax, fugacis evasive, fleeting, fleeing

habena, -ae, *f.* rein, strap, cord

interritus, -a, -um fearless, not terrified

Ligus, -uris, *m.* a Ligurian, an inhabitant of Cisalpine Gaul

lubricus, -a, -um slippery, inconstant

nequiquam *adv.* in vain, uselessly

nudus, -a, -um naked, bare, exposed

parma, -ae, *f.* shield

pedes, peditis, *m.* foot-soldier, infantryman

purus, -a, -um clean, pure, free of decoration, unadorned, plain

quadripes, quadripedis (or **quadru-**) four-footed; (*used as a noun*) *m.* a four-footed animal

resisto, -ere, restiti resist, stop, pause, stand firm

trado, -ere, tradidi, traditus hand over, hand down

vanus, -a, -um false, groundless, unreliable, foolish

710–11. **comiti**: i.e., one of the female warriors who follows her. **paribus ... in armis**: i.e., Camilla accepts the Ligurian's challenge and dismounts; she is now equipped much like her opponent. **ense ... nudo puraque ... parma**: a nice CHIASMUS, with the two epithets virtual synonyms. **pedes**: in apposition with Camilla, the implied subject of **resistit**.

712. **vicisse**: perf. act. inf. in indir. statement after **ratus**; **se** is its implied subject. **dolo**: abl. of means. Note the repeated emphasis on trickery throughout this scene. **avolat ipse**: now that he has succeeded in his challenge to Camilla to dismount, the Ligurian quickly mounts his horse and flies

off; his intent is to leave Camilla standing in the dust.

713. **haud mora (est). conversis ... habenis**: abl. abs. or abl. of means.

714. **quadripedem**: a lofty equivalent for **equum** that enhances the ONOMATOPOEIA of the description. **ferrata calce**: abl. of means.

715. **Vane Ligus ... elate**: voc. **frustra**: modifies **elate**. **animis ... superbis**: abl. of means or description.

716. **patrias ... artes**: Camilla knows that trickery is characteristic of the Ligurians. **temptasti**: syncopated perf. = **temptavisti**. **lubricus**: in apposition to **tu**, the implied subject of **temptasti**.

nec fraus te incolumem fallaci perferet Auno." ·
haec fatur virgo, et pernicibus ignea plantis
transit equum cursu frenisque adversa prehensis
720   congreditur poenasque inimico ex sanguine sumit:
quam facile accipiter saxo sacer ales ab alto
consequitur pennis sublimem in nube columbam

---

accipiter, accipitris, *m.* hawk

adversus, -a, -um turned towards, facing, opposite

ales, alitis, *m./f.* large bird, bird of prey

Aunus, -i, *m.* Aunus, a man from the mountains of northern Italy

columba, -ae, *f.* dove

congredior, congredi, congressus meet, approach

consequor, consequi, consecutus pursue, overtake

facile *adv.* easily

fallax, fallacis deceitful, lying

fraus, fraudis, *f.* harm, danger; deceit

frenum, -i, *n.* rein, bridle

igneus, -a, -um burning, fiery, ardent

incolumis, -e safe, unharmed

inimicus, -a, -um hostile, unfriendly

penna, -ae, *f.* wing

perfero, perferre, pertuli, perlatus carry, bring, convey

pernix, pernicis swift, speedy

planta, -ae, *f.* sole (of the foot); tread, walking, step

prehendo, -ere, prehendi, prehensus grasp, sieze, take hold of

sublimis, -e high, elevated, aloft

sumo, -ere, sumpsi, sumptus take up, take possession of; (+ **poenas**) exact (a penalty)

transeo, -ire, transii *or* **transivi, transitus** go across, go past, pass

---

717. **nec ... te incolumem**: LITOTES; the thinly veiled threat may be meant to recall the funeral of Pallas, described earlier in Book 11. **fraus**: Camilla cleverly turns the Ligurian's own expertise against him. **fallaci ... Auno**: once again she notes that he is no better than his father. **perferet**: cf. the use of the fut. in 708.

718. **pernicibus ... plantis**: abl. of description or means. **ignea**: a strong reminder of her rage and passion for battle, as well as a METAPHOR for her swiftness.

719. **transit equum cursu**: running, she passes his horse. Camilla's swiftness on foot is a distinctive feature of her description earlier in the *Aeneid*, at Book 7.807–11. **frenis ... prehensis**: abl. abs.

721–24. Vergil uses a SIMILE (more precisely, half of a SIMILE; the part that would normally make the comparison explicit is suppressed) at the climax of his description of the defeat of the Ligurian by Camilla; visually effective, the device also serves here to direct our attention to the heavens where the two birds in the SIMILE fight. In the subsequent lines, the action will shift briefly to Jupiter, who sits observing the war.

721. **quam**: introduces the SIMILE. **accipiter ... sacer ... ales**: Camilla is compared to a hawk sacred to Jupiter; her victory seems therefore entirely predictable.

722. **pennis**: abl. of means or description. **columbam**: an odd choice for comparison with the crafty Ligurian, yet the dove is clearly no match for the hawk.

comprensamque tenet pedibusque eviscerat uncis;
tum cruor et vulsae labuntur ab aethere plumae.

---

comprendo (*or* **comprehendo**), **-ere,
compr(eh)endi, compr(eh)ensus** take
hold of, grip, hold
cruor, cruoris, *m.* blood
eviscero (1) disembowel, eviscerate

pluma, -ae, *f.* feather
uncus, -a, -um curved, hooked
vello, -ere, velli, vulsus pull out, pull up,
extract, tear

---

723. **pedibus ... uncis**: abl. of means.
eviscerat: the verb leaves little to the imagi-
nation.

725–67. After this victory, Vergil shifts his (and our) attention briefly from Camilla, and focuses on the opposing troops led by the Etruscan Tarchon. (Vergil tells in Book 10 of the various Etruscan and allied groups who agree to support the Trojan cause and Evander; Tarchon is first among them.) This scene offers many parallels to that which preceded it; it also delays for a while longer Camilla's final challenge and defeat.

725   At non haec nullis hominum sator atque deorum
           observans oculis summo sedet altus Olympo.
           Tyrrhenum genitor Tarchonem in proelia saeva
           suscitat et stimulis haud mollibus incitat iras.
           Ergo inter caedes cedentiaque agmina Tarchon
730   fertur equo variisque instigat vocibus alas
           nomine quemque vocans, reficitque in proelia pulsos.

---

ala, -ae, *f.* wing; band or troop of warriors, wing of an army

caedes, -is, *f.* slaughter, killing

incito (1) set in motion, provoke, rouse

instigo (1) incite, impel, urge on, stir up

mollis, -e gentle, soft, mild, tender

observo (1) observe, take notice of, watch

Olympus, -i, *m.* Olympus, home of the gods

pello, -ere, pepuli, pulsus strike, beat, drive, impel

proelium, -i, *n.* battle, conflict

quisque, quaeque, quidque each

reficio, -ere, refeci, refectus repair, restore, renew

sator, satoris, *m.* sower, begetter, progenitor

stimulus, -i, *m.* goad, prick, spur, provocation

suscito (1) stir, rouse, arouse

Tarchon, Tarchonis, *m.* Tarchon, Etruscan leader, ally of Aeneas

Tyrrhenus, -a, -um Etruscan, Tyrrhenian

725–26. **At:** the scene (i.e., the perspective of the viewer) now shifts to Olympus. **non ... nullis ... oculis:** a true double negative (LITOTES). **hominum sator atque deorum:** Jupiter.

727. **Tyrrhenum genitor Tarchonem:** the placement of **genitor** suggests that Jupiter is Tarchon's father, although there is no indication of this elsewhere in Vergil.

728. **stimulis haud mollibus:** abl. of means; LITOTES.

730. **equo:** abl. of place or means. **variis ... vocibus:** abl. of means.

731. **nomine:** abl. of means. It is a mark of a good leader that Tarchon knows each of his men's names and so can encourage each man personally. **in proelia:** here, the acc. with **in** expresses purpose.

732–40. Tarchon's speech to his men is psychologically shrewd: he neither consoles them for their losses nor acknowledges their wounds, but mocks them for their poor showing against a woman and implies that they are more interested in pleasure and comfort than in their own honor.

"Quis metus, o numquam dolituri, o semper inertes
Tyrrheni, quae tanta animis ignavia venit?
Femina palantes agit atque haec agmina vertit!
Quo ferrum quidve haec gerimus tela inrita dextris?   735
At non in Venerem segnes nocturnaque bella,
aut ubi curva choros indixit tibia Bacchi.
exspectate dapes et plenae pocula mensae

Bacchus, -i, *m.* Bacchus, god of wine

chorus, -i, *m.* chorus, troupe

curvus, -a, -um curved, winding, tortuous, twisting

daps, dapis, *f.* feast, banquet

doleo, -ere, dolui grieve, be in pain, feel grief, feel sorrow

exspecto (1) wait for, expect, look forward to

ignavia, -ae, *f.* sloth, lack of spirit

indico, -ere, indixi, indictum announce, proclaim

iners, inertis lazy, inactive, spiritless

inritus, -a, -um unfulfilled, ineffectual, bringing no result

nocturnus, -a, -um nocturnal, belonging to the night

numquam *adv.* never

palor, palari, palatus wander, scatter, stray

plenus, -a, -um full

poculum, -i, *n.* cup

segnis, -e lazy, slothful, sluggish

semper *adv.* always

tibia, -ae, *f.* pipe, reed instrument

Venus, Veneris, *f.* Venus, goddess of love; love

732–33. Quis metus, ... quae tanta ... ignavia: Tarchon postpones the most embarrassing feature of their performance on the battlefield for last. **o numquam dolituri, o semper inertes Tyrrheni:** voc. pl. **dolituri:** Tarchon's point is not that they *will* never feel pain—indeed, many of them have done so already; rather, he uses the fut. act. participle here to characterize them as *intent upon* never feeling pain. **animis:** dat. of direction with **venit**.

734. (vos) palantes: the verb **palor** is not complimentary—it appears most frequently in Latin literature to describe either the behavior of defeated troops or the unregulated movement of heavenly bodies.

735. quo ... quidve: two ways of asking *for what reason*? Understand **gerimus** as the verb in both rhetorical questions.

736. in Venerem ... nocturnaque bella: acc. of purpose or intent with **in. Venerem:** metonymy for all things associated with Venus, especially love affairs and sex. **nocturna ... bella:** a familiar metaphor from Latin love elegy for the "battles" that form a part of the game of seduction; here, used in apt contrast to the real battles that, Tarchon implies, these men shun.

737. choros ... tibia Bacchi: three Greek nouns in a single line are used effectively to characterize the implicitly unheroic indulgence of Tarchon's men, especially given their meaning: the first two are associated with music and dance, the third is the name of the god who presides over festive abandonment (and is used here both literally and as a metonymy for the god's gift of wine).

738. exspectate: pl. imperative.

(hic amor, hoc studium) dum sacra secundus haruspex
740 nuntiet ac lucos vocet hostia pinguis in altos!"
Haec effatus equum in medios moriturus et ipse
concitat, et Venulo adversum se turbidus infert
dereptumque ab equo dextra complectitur hostem
et gremium ante suum multa vi concitus aufert.
745 Tollitur in caelum clamor, cunctique Latini

---

adversus, -a, -um turned towards, facing, opposite

complector, complecti, complexus embrace, clasp, cling to

concieo, -ere, concivi, concitus stir up, excite

concito (1) spur, urge on, stir

deripio, -ere, deripui, dereptus pull off, grab, snatch off

effor, effari, effatus say, speak, utter

gremium, -i, *n.* lap

haruspex, haruspicis, *m.* diviner, interpreter of omens

hostia, -ae, *f.* sacrificial animal, sacrificial victim

infero, inferre, intuli, illatus carry in, bring, impel

morior, mori, mortuus die

nuntio (1) announce, report

pinguis, -e rich, fat, fertile, plump

studium, -i, *n.* inclination, zeal, pursuit, desire

turbidus, -a, -um agitated, troubled, confused, in turmoil

Venulus, -i, *m.* Venulus, comrade of Turnus

739–40. **hic amor, hoc studium (est)**: emphatic combination of ANAPHORA and ASYNDETON. **nuntiet ac … vocet**: pres. subjunctives in a clause of anticipation introduced by **dum**, expressing something that is anticipated but has not happened yet. **dum … altos**: the scene Tarchon imagines is of a propitious reading of the omens and a rich sacrifice performed in a sacred grove—both of which, he implies, may well not happen if his men do not turn the tide of battle soon. **vocet** (**vos** *or* **nos**).

741. **moriturus et ipse**: Vergil underscores the irony of the speech Tarchon has just given: a leader cannot expect to survive for sacrifices and feasts after the war. Curiously, however, Vergil never describes Tarchon's death in the *Aeneid*. The participle is therefore not necessarily a statement of fact, but an indication of Tarchon's willingness to die.

742. **Venulo**: dat. of direction with **se** … **infert** or dat. of reference with **adversum**. Venulus is identified elsewhere as one of Aeneas' highly trusted emissaries. **adversum**: most likely adverbial here, although it can also be interpreted as adj. followed by dat. of reference. **turbidus**: i.e., like a **turbo** (*whirlwind*) or **turba** (*mass of confusion*).

743. **dextra**: abl. of means.

744. **gremium ante suum**: the unusual word order emphasizes the oddness of the position Venulus is in; earlier in this book (11.544), Metabus is described as carrying the infant Camilla before him as he flees to protect her. **multa vi**: abl. of means or manner.

745. **tollitur in caelum clamor**: again Vergil marks a change of perspective, as the entire army of Latins turns to see and to exclaim at the evident success of Tarchon.

convertere oculos. Volat igneus aequore Tarchon
arma virumque ferens; tum summa ipsius ab hasta
defringit ferrum et partes rimatur apertas,
qua vulnus letale ferat; contra ille repugnans
sustinet a iugulo dextram et vim viribus exit.   750
Utque volans alte raptum cum fulva draconem
fert aquila implicuitque pedes atque unguibus haesit,

---

aquila, -ae, *f.* eagle

converto, -ere, converti, conversus turn,
    turn towards

defringo, -ere, defregi, defractus break
    off

draco, draconis, *m.* snake

exeo, exire, exii *or* exivi, exitus go out;
    elude, escape

fulvus, -a, -um tawny

hasta, -ae, *f.* spear, javelin

igneus, -a, -um burning, fiery, ardent

implico, -are, implicui, implicatus enfold,
    wrap inside, entwine

iugulum, -i, *n.* neck, throat

letalis, -e deadly, lethal

repugno (1) fight back, defend, offer
    resistance

rimor, rimari, rimatus search out,
    examine, scrutinize

sustineo, -ere, sustinui lift, support;
    check, withstand; keep from

unguis, -is, *m.* claw, talon

volo (1) fly, move swiftly

---

746. **convertere**: alternate third pers. pl.
perf. **volat igneus aequore Tarchon**: the
metaphorical language here recalls the de-
scription of Camilla in 11.718–24. **aequore**:
This word, commonly defined as meaning
"sea," describes any flat surface, including
but not limited to that of the sea. Here, the
broad battlefield is meant. See also 10.444.

747. **arma virumque**: another allusion
to the opening line of the *Aeneid*, here ap-
plied to Tarchon; at 11.596, it characterized
Camilla. **summa ... ab hasta**: abl. of separa-
tion. **ipsius**: i.e., of Venulus, owner of the
spear.

748. **defringit ferrum**: Tarchon breaks
the iron blade off the spear shaft. **partes
rimatur apertas**: Tarchon seeks a place on
Venulus' body that is not protected by ar-
mor and is therefore vulnerable.

749. **qua**: opens an indir. question whose
introductory verb (e.g., **petit, quaerit**) is
implied. **ferat**: pres. subjunctive in an in-
dir. question; its subject is Tarchon. **contra
ille**: the adv. and demonstrative together

now direct our attention from Tarchon to
Venulus, who is struggling to escape from
his captor.

750. **sustinet a iugulo (suo) (eius) dex-
tram**: i.e., Venulus pushes Tarchon's hand
from his own neck. **vim viribus exit**: a
highly unusual transitive use of the verb;
here, translate, *he evades (Tarchon's) force
with force.*

751–58. As in the preceding struggle
between Camilla and the Ligurian, here
too Vergil brings the struggle between
two warriors to a vivid conclusion with a
SIMILE.

751–52. **utque ... cum**: the conjunction is
postponed, as often in the opening of SIMI-
LES. **raptum ... fulva draconem ... aquila**:
SYNCHYSIS aptly illustrates the relationship
between the flying eagle and the coiling
snake it carries; the picture evoked by the
word order is then made explicit with the
following verb, **implicuit**. **pedes**: i.e., the
eagle's own feet are curved around the
snake. **unguibus**: abl. of means.

saucius at serpens sinuosa volumina versat
arrectisque horret squamis et sibilat ore
755   arduus insurgens, illa haud minus urget obunco
luctantem rostro, simul aethera verberat alis:
haud aliter praedam Tiburtum ex agmine Tarchon
portat ovans. Ducis exemplum eventumque secuti
Maeonidae incurrunt. Tum fatis debitus Arruns

---

aliter *adv.* otherwise, differently
arrigo, -ere, arrexi, arrectus stand up straight
Arruns, Arruntis, *m.* Arruns, an Etruscan
debeo, -ere, debui, debitus owe, ought
eventus, -us, *m.* outcome, result
exemplum, -i, *n.* example
incurro, -ere, incurri, incursus rush, charge at, run in
insurgo, -ere, insurrexi rise, extend up
luctor, luctari, luctatus wrestle, struggle
Maeonidae, -arum, *m. pl.* Etruscans
minus *adv.* less, to a smaller extent
obuncus, -a, -um hooked, curved
ovo (1) rejoice, exult
porto (1) carry

praeda, -ae, *f.* booty, spoils, prize
rostrum, -i, *n.* beak
saucius, -a, -um wounded
serpens, serpentis, *m.(f.)* snake, serpent
sibilo (1) hiss
sinuosus, -a, -um bending, curving, twisting
squama, -ae, *f.* scale
Tiburs, Tiburtis belonging to Tibur; inhabitant of Tibur
urgeo, -ere, ursi press, urge
verbero (1) beat, strike, batter
verso (1) turn, turn over, keep turning over, revolve, ponder
volumen, voluminis, *n.* roll, coil, twist

---

753. **saucius at serpens**: the postponed **at** is strongly adversative. ALLITERATION is a favorite feature in Vergil's descriptions of snakes.

754. **arrectis … squamis**: abl. abs. **sibilat**: the verb expresses the sound effects of these lines. **ore**: abl. of source or means.

755–56. **arduus insurgens**: the linking of two epithets without any conjunction is unusual and striking: comparable is the description of Camilla at 11.697, **altior exsurgens**, as she rises to strike with her battle-axe. **illa**: the eagle; the demonstrative used with no connective (ASYNDETON) marks the contrast. **obunco … rostro**: abl. of means. **luctantem**: i.e., the snake. **alis**: abl. of means.

757. **haud aliter**: the SIMILE comes to a close as the explicit comparison is drawn. **Tiburtum ex agmine**: a subtle reminder

of Camilla's relevance to this scene, as she was entrusted by Turnus with the leadership of the Tiburtines at 11.519. **Tiburtum**: gen. pl.

758. **ovans**: parading in triumph.

759. **Maeonidae**: Maeonia was an ancient name for Lydia in Asia Minor, from which, tradition had it, the Etruscans had come; Vergil uses this patronymic ("the descendants of Maeonia") only here in the *Aeneid*. **Tum … Arruns**: this character, otherwise unknown, plays a crucial role in this scene; yet his introduction in mid-hexameter is abrupt and unexpected, just like him. **fatis debitus**: this foreshadowing leaves little doubt that Arruns will bring Camilla's doom, though how he will do so remains to be seen. Vergil also reminds us subtly here of Diana's vow that the killer of Camilla will pay the penalty (11.591–92).

velocem iaculo et multa prior arte Camillam 760
circuit, et quae sit fortuna facillima temptat.
Qua se cumque furens medio tulit agmine virgo,
hac Arruns subit et tacitus vestigia lustrat;
qua victrix redit illa pedemque ex hoste reportat,
hac iuvenis furtim celeres detorquet habenas. 765
Hos aditus iamque hos aditus omnemque pererrat
undique circuitum et certam quatit improbus hastam.

---

aditus, -us, *m.* approach, entrance, pass
circu(m)eo, circu(m)ire, circu(m)ii,
 circu(m)itus go around, coil around,
 surround, encircle
circu(m)itus, -us, *m.* orbit, cycle, perimeter
detorqueo, -ere, detorsi, detortus turn
 away, deflect, change direction
facilis, -e easy, straightforward
furtim *adv.* secretly, furtively
habena, -ae, *f.* rein, strap, cord
hasta, -ae, *f.* spear, javelin
iaculum, -i, *n.* javelin
improbus, -a, -um unprincipled,
 shameless, presumptuous, wicked

pererro (1) wander through, traverse,
 meander
quacumque *adv.* by whatever way,
 wherever
quatio, -ere, —, quassus shake, disturb,
 cause to tremble, brandish
redeo, redire, redii *or* **redivi, reditus**
 return, go back
reporto (1) carry back, bring back
tacitus, -a, -um silent
velox, velocis swift, rapid speedy
victrix, victricis, *f.* conqueror, victorious
 one

---

760. **iaculo et ... multa ... arte**: abl. of
description or specification. **prior (ei)**: i.e.,
Arruns is superior to Camilla in these strat-
agems of war.

761. **quae sit fortuna facillima**: indir.
question introduced by **temptat**.

762. **Qua se cumque**: TMESIS; **se** is reflex-
ive acc. with **tulit**. **medio ... agmine**: abl.
of place.

763. **hac**: abl. of place; corresponds to **qua**
in the preceding line. **tacitus**: modifies the
implied subject, Arruns.

764–65. **qua**: echoes in abbreviated form
the **quacumque** of 762; the repetition,

which continues with **hac** in the following
line; evokes the slow, studied stalking of
Camilla by Arruns. **iuvenis**: Arruns.

766–67. **Hos aditus iamque hos aditus**:
the verbal repetition, like that of **qua/hoc** in
the four lines preceding, captures Arruns'
indefatigable search for a way to get to Ca-
milla. *omnem ... pererrat undique circui-*
tum: note the emphasis on thoroughness
as Arruns circles Camilla; the noun **circui-**
tum echoes the first verb used of Arruns,
circuit (761), and so evokes Arruns' circular
course from which there will be no escape.
improbus: in apposition to Arruns.

768–93. In the preceding lines, Arruns has stalked Camilla obsessively but without result; now an opportunity presents itself, in the person of the Phrygian Chloreus, for Arruns to gain the closer access to Camilla he needs. Chloreus, formerly a priest of Cybele, wears remarkable garb—so remarkable indeed that it distracts Camilla from the other warriors on the battlefield. Her inattention gives Arruns an opening at last.

> Forte sacer Cybelo Chloreus olimque sacerdos
> insignis longe Phrygiis fulgebat in armis

Chloreus, -i *or* **-ei,** *m.* Chloreus, an ally of Aeneas

Cybelus, -i, *m.* Cybelus (or Cybele), a mountain in Phrygia sacred to the goddess Cybele

fulgeo, -ere, fulsi, fulsus gleam, shine, glitter

insignis, -e notable, distinguished

olim *adv.* formerly, once

Phrygius, -a, -um Phrygian, Trojan

---

768. **Forte**: Vergil makes prominent the ironic role of chance in Camilla's demise. **Cybelo**: dat. with **sacer**. Cybelus is the name of the mountain in Asia Minor upon which the worship of the goddess Cybele was centered. The worship of Cybele (also called Magna Mater by the Romans) was a unique phenomenon in the Roman world: originally a Near Eastern goddess, she was brought to Rome in 204 BCE, when the Romans feared defeat by Hannibal in the Second Punic War and so solicited as much divine aid as possible. Her Roman cult was centered at a temple on the Palatine hill (close to the site where Augustus would eventually locate his own dwelling); while the Roman population as a whole thereafter enjoyed the games (Megalensia) celebrated in her honor every April, only men of Near Eastern origin could enter her priesthood. This prohibition is most likely related to the fact that Cybele's priests were castrated; indeed, various versions of her myth indicate that her priests castrated themselves while in an ecstatic trance provoked by her worship. Chloreus' appearance on the battlefield is therefore especially remarkable:

with Camilla and Chloreus, Vergil juxtaposes two characters whose presence on the battlefield poses a challenge to the gender distinctions usually ascribed to Roman men and women. **Chloreus**: the unusual name is etymologically linked to the Greek word for *green* or *greenish yellow*; it thus anticipates the colorful description to follow. Note that the name consists of two long syllables; the combination **-eu-** is pronounced as one sound through SYNIZESIS. **olimque sacerdos**: the phrase is somewhat puzzling—does Vergil mean that Chloreus had been a priest of Cybele, but is no longer? If so, it is difficult to imagine how Chloreus could have relinquished his priesthood, especially if, as is likely, we are to imagine that he castrated himself as part of the process of entering the priesthood. It is furthermore most unusual to hear of priesthoods with term limits in the Roman world. **olim** cannot mean "for a long time now"; it is most likely, therefore, that Vergil means us to think of Chloreus as having been a priest in the cult center on Mt. Cybelus, but now acting outside his priestly role as a warrior on the battlefield.

spumantemque agitabat equum, quem pellis aënis   770
in plumam squamis auro conserta tegebat.
Ipse peregrina ferrugine clarus et ostro
spicula torquebat Lycio Gortynia cornu;
aureus ex umeris erat arcus et aurea vati
cassida; tum croceam chlamydemque sinusque crepantes   775
carbaseos fulvo in nodum collegerat auro

---

aënus, -a, -um of bronze, brazen
arcus, -us, *m.* bow
carbaseus, -a, -um made of linen
cassida, -ae, *f.* helmet
chlamys, chlamydis, *f.* cloak, cape
colligo, -ere, collegi, collectus gather together, gather
consero, -ere, conserui, consertus connect, join, fasten together
cornu, cornus, *n.* horn, ivory; bow
crepo (1) rustle, crackle, rattle
croceus, -a, -um saffron-colored, yellow
ferrugo, ferruginis, *f.* rust, rust-colored
fulvus, -a, -um tawny

Gortynius, -a, -um of or belonging to Gortynia, Gortynian, Cretan
Lycius, -a, -um of or belonging to Lycia, Lycian
nodus, -i, *m.* knot
ostrum, -i, *n.* purple color, purple
pellis, -is, *f.* skin, hide
peregrinus, -a, -um foreign
pluma, -ae, *f.* feather
sinus, -us, *m.* fold; bosom; embrace
spiculum, -i, *n.* point of a weapon, arrow
squama, -ae, *f.* scale
tego, -ere, texi, tectus cover

770–71. The description of the covering worn by Chloreus' horse is complex—part armor and part decoration, its exotic features are paralleled by Vergil's distorted word order. **pellis ... auro conserta:** the horse wears an animal hide interwoven with gold thread; **auro** is abl. of material. **aënis ... squamis:** abl. of description. **in plumam: in** + acc. is used to express purpose; "with bronze scales [formed] into *or* for plumage." Note the placement of the prep. phrase between the two words that provide its context. **tegebat:** the verb in the rel. clause; its subject is **pellis.**

772. **peregrina ferrugine ... et ostro:** abl. of description and/or specification. The deep red and purple of his garments are another mark of his exotic nature.

773. **spicula ... Lycio Gortynia cornu:** SYNCHYSIS. Both the Lycians (a people of Asia Minor) and the Gortynians (people from an area on the Greek island of Crete) were famed as archers.

774. **aureus ... aurea:** the repeated emphasis on gold reflects Camilla's perspective. **ex umeris:** abl. of separation; understand, e.g., **dependens. vati:** dat. of reference.

775–76. **cassida:** an uncommon word, appropriate for non-Roman headgear. **croceam chlamydemque sinusque crepantes:** CHIASMUS and POLYSYNDETON (or HENDIADYS: the phrase is equivalent to **croceae chlamydis sinus crepantes**) enhance the elaborate picture. **sinus crepantes carbaseos:** the lack of connective between the adjs. (ASYNDETON) emphasizes the overabundance of fabric in Chloreus' rich dress. **fulvo in nodum ... auro: in** + acc. again expresses purpose ("gathered into/for the purpose of a knot"); the object with which the knot is held (perhaps a sort of brooch, although Vergil is not specific) is expressed as an abl. of material or description. Note the third reference to gold in three lines, and the placement of **auro** at the end of its verse and after the verb: the effect is emphatic and ominous, as we are again reminded of Camilla's perspective.

pictus acu tunicas et barbara tegmina crurum.
Hunc virgo, sive ut templis praefigeret arma
Troia, captivo sive ut se ferret in auro
780   venatrix, unum ex omni certamine pugnae
caeca sequebatur totumque incauta per agmen
femineo praedae et spoliorum ardebat amore,

---

acus, -us, *f.* needle

barbarus, -a, -um foreign

captivus, -a, -um captured in war, captive

crus, cruris, *n.* leg, shin

femineus, -a, -um womanly, belonging to a woman, woman's

incautus, -a, -um not cautious, careless

pingo, -ere, pinxi, pinctus paint, decorate, adorn, embroider

praefigo, -ere, praefixi, praefixus attach, fasten

spolium, -i, *n.* spoils, booty

tegmen, tegminis, *n.* covering

tunica, -ae, *f.* tunic

venatrix, venatricis, *f.* female hunter

---

777. **pictus**: perf. pass. participle, modifying **Chloreus**, the implied subject of **collegerat**; it is used as if it were a Greek middle participle capable of taking an acc. obj., here **tunicas et barbara tegmina**. Thus, we may understand the acc. objs. as acc. of respect in the so-called Greek acc. construction, lit., *having been embroidered with respect to tunics and the barbarian coverings for legs*. A simpler translation would be *wearing tunics embroidered with a needle and barbarian leg-coverings*. **acu**: abl. of means. **barbara tegmina crurum**: the wearing of trousers was considered by the Romans to be a mark of the barbarian.

778–79. **Hunc**: i.e., Chloreus; dir. obj. of **sequebatur** (781). **sive ut … sive ut**: a double purpose clause, each of whose vbs. is in the impf. subjunctive. By providing alternative reasons, Vergil suggests that Camilla's motives are unclear and the subject of possible debate. **templis praefigeret arma**: a standard way of showing thanks to the gods for their help on the battlefield; presumably, the temple of Diana is the intended recipient. **Troia**: here, a trisyllable, scanned as a dactyl. **captivo … in auro**: not captive gold, but gold that has been captured from a defeated enemy; Vergil imagines that Camilla may be motivated by the desire to wear the golden spoils taken from Chloreus, and so

provides a context for the emphasis on gold in the preceding lines.

780. **venatrix**: ENJAMBMENT. As the last word in its clause, this emphatic epithet may be intended to suggest other hunters and hunting scenes in the *Aeneid*; cf. in particular the description of Dido at 4.136–39, as she emerges from her bedchamber to embark on the hunt with Aeneas. **unum**: modifies **hunc** (778). The two adjs. surround the double purpose clause and so suggest not only the important presence of Chloreus in distracting Camilla but also that of Arruns, as he lurks and stalks her. **unum ex omni certamine**: partitive with **ex** + abl.

781. **caeca … incauta**: modifying the implied subject of **sequebatur**, Camilla. **caeca … totumque incauta per agmen**: INTERLOCKING WORD ORDER/ SYNCHYSIS.

782. **femineo praedae et spoliorum …amore**: CHIASMUS. **femineo … amore**: scholars have long wondered whether the epithet is intended to be negative and dismissive, or simply reflects a cliché, seen frequently elsewhere in Latin literature, that women are (sometimes excessively) fond of gold jewelry. Yet the love of and admiration for gold are hardly exclusive to Roman women; gold spoils and booty in particular might well be considered an exclusively male prerogative. **praedae et spoliorum**: objective gen.

telum ex insidiis cum tandem tempore capto
concitat et superos Arruns sic voce precatur:
"Summe deum, sancti custos Soractis Apollo,   785
quem primi colimus, cui pineus ardor acervo
pascitur, et medium freti pietate per ignem
cultores multa premimus vestigia pruna,

---

acervus, -i, *m.* heap, pile

ardor, ardoris, *m.* burning, fire, conflagration

concito (1) set in motion, hurl, urge on, rouse

cultor, cultoris, *m.* inhabitant, worshipper

fretus, -a, -um relying on, confident in

insidiae, -arum, *f. pl.* ambush, surprise attack, plot

sanctus, -a, -um sacred, holy, inviolate

Soracte, -is, *n.* Soracte, a mountain in Etruria

pascor, pasci, pastus feed, pasture, nourish

pineus, -a, -um of pine, made of pine-wood

pruna, -ae, *f.* live coal, hot ash

783–84. Virtually every detail in the first of these lines creates suspense: as the first word in the line, **telum** creates a vivid image of threat, but no agent is named; **ex insidiis** confirms the reader's suspicion that Camilla is in danger, and further points to Arruns without naming him; **cum tandem** marks what is to happen next as climactic; and **tempore capto** fixes this as the crucial moment. Vergil postpones naming Arruns, and so bringing him to the fore, until after the caesura in the second of these lines, when at last he takes center stage for his sole speech in the *Aeneid*. **telum**: acc. **cum ... concitat et ... precatur**: cum is temporal with the indicative. **tempore capto**: abl. abs. **voce**: abl. of means.

785. **Summe**: voc.; both a term of praise and an allusion to the mountain heights on which Apollo is worshipped. **deum**: gen. pl.; partitive gen. **sancti ... Soractis**: an isolated and impressive mountain north of Rome, very noticeable on the horizon at a height of 691 meters (2,267 feet). In *Odes* 1.9, Vergil's contemporary Horace offers a memorable vignette of looking towards the snowy peaks of Soracte from the snug warmth of an indoor setting. Arruns' interest is in Soracte as the site of a shrine of Apollo (where, we shall see, an unusual form of

worship is practiced): as he tracks Camilla, Arruns prays for help to Apollo as the god of sudden death and destruction. Apollo was the divinity perhaps most favored by Augustus (see my comments on Book 8, esp. lines 704 and 720); in aligning Arruns with Apollo, therefore, Vergil reminds us that Arruns' purpose is to ensure the eventual foundation of Rome by Aeneas.

786. **quem ... cui**: the antecedent in each case is Apollo. **(nos) primi**: nom. pl. Arruns refers to himself and his fellow worshippers. **cui**: dat. of reference. **pineus ardor**: abstract for concrete noun. **acervo**: abl. of specification.

787–88. Arruns describes the unusual ritual of walking on hot coals practiced by Apollo's followers on Soracte. Pliny refers briefly to the same practice in his *Encyclopedia* (*NH* 7.19), where he identifies the Hirpi, a family well known in the area of Soracte, as its practitioners; but there is otherwise little evidence for this activity. Scholars have, however, studied similar rituals involving immunity to fire in many other religions, in both the classical world and elsewhere. **pietate**: abl. with **freti**. **multa ... pruna**: abl. of place or of description. **premimus**: its subject is **freti ... cultores**; its dir. obj. is **vestigia**.

790   da, pater, hoc nostris aboleri dedecus armis,
omnipotens. Non exuvias pulsaeve tropaeum
virginis aut spolia ulla peto, mihi cetera laudem
facta ferent; haec dira meo dum vulnere pestis
pulsa cadat, patrias remeabo inglorius urbes."

---

aboleo, -ere, abolevi, abolitus destroy,
wipe out

ceterus, -a, -um the rest, the remaining

dedecus, dedecoris, *n.* shame, dishonor,
disgrace

exuviae, -arum, *f. pl.* armor, spoils; skin
stripped from dead beast

factum, -i, *n.* deed, action, act

inglorius, -a, -um undistinguished,
unhonored

omnipotens, omnipotentis all powerful,
omnipotent

pello, -ere, pepuli, pulsus strike, beat,
drive, impel

pestis, pestis, *f.* plague, curse, pest

remeo (1) return, go back

spolium, -i, *n.* spoils, booty

tropaeum, -i, *n.* trophy, victory

---

789. **da**: this imperative introduces an
acc. + inf. rather than the indir. command
we might expect in prose. The grammar of
Vergil's prayer-form is archaic and ritualis-
tic, as are prayers themselves. **hoc ... abo-
leri dedecus**: acc. + pres. pass. inf. Rather
than naming her or identifying her direct-
ly, Arruns describes Camilla only through
an abstract noun; contrast with Turnus' ad-
dress to Camilla as **decus Italiae** (11.508).
nostris ... armis: abl. of means.

790–93. **omnipotens**: VOC.; ENJAMBMENT.
non ... peto: we may be sure that Arruns'
apparent self-denial is no hardship; he
knows well what people will say of him if
he takes spoils from a female warrior. **exu-
vias, tropaeum, spolia**: Arruns effectively
says the same thing three times to empha-
size how little he cares for the spoils of war.

mihi: the lack of connective (ASYNDETON) is
strongly adversative. **cetera ... facta**: Vergil-
ian irony, since Arruns will soon disappear
from the narrative (815), only to reappear
for his ignoble death at 11.864–67. **ferent**:
fut. indicative is a misplaced assertion of
certainty here. **haec dira ... pestis**: again
Arruns uses a METAPHOR to refer indirectly
to Camilla. In calling her a "dread plague,"
he uses language elsewhere applied by
Vergil to the powerful effects of the Fury
Allecto (*Aeneid* Book 7). **meo ... vulnere**:
i.e., the wound caused by me; abl. of means
with **pulsa**. **dum ... cadat**: subjunctive with
dum expresses anticipation or proviso
rather than fact. **remeabo inglorius**: the
adj. modifies the subject of the verb; fut. in-
dicative again lays claim to a certainty on
Arruns' part lacking in Vergil's text.

794–815. With Apollo's help, Arruns strikes the fatal blow; he then escapes into the confusion on the battlefield.

> Audiit et voti Phoebus succedere partem
> mente dedit, partem volucres dispersit in auras: 795
> sterneret ut subita turbatam morte Camillam
> adnuit oranti; reducem ut patria alta videret
> non dedit, inque Notos vocem vertere procellae.
> Ergo ut missa manu sonitum dedit hasta per auras,
> convertere animos acres oculosque tulere 800
> cuncti ad reginam Volsci. Nihil ipsa nec aurae
> nec sonitus memor aut venientis ab aethere teli,

---

adnuo, -ere, adnui, adnutus approve, nod approval, grant

converto, -ere, converti, conversus turn, turn towards

dispergo, -ere, dispersi, dispersus scatter, disperse

memor, memoris mindful, aware, remembering

nihil, *n. indecl.* nothing, not, not at all

Notus, -i, *m.* Notus, the south wind

patria, -ae, *f.* country, home-land

Phoebus, -i, *m.* a name for Apollo, Apollo

procella, -ae, *f.* blast, storm, storm-wind

redux, reducis returning, coming home

succedo, -ere, successi, successus advance, succeed, turn out well

turbo (1) agitate, disturb, confuse, upset

Volsci, -orum, *m. pl.* Volscians, a people of Latium

votum, -i, *n.* vow, promise, prayer

794–95. **succedere partem ... dedit:** acc. + inf. after **dedit**, corresponding to the construction of Arruns' request in 789. **partem ... partem:** construe **voti** with each instance of the word. **volucres ... in auras:** acc. of motion towards; the winds are traditionally responsible for snatching words spoken in vain.

796–97. **sterneret ut:** ANASTROPHE. The subject of the verb is Arruns; this clause corresponds to the first part of his prayer (i.e., the part granted by Apollo). **ut:** introduces a substantive clause of purpose (alternatively, indir. command) following **oranti (Arrunti). subita turbatam morte Camillam:** SYNCHYSIS. **oranti:** dat. with **adnuit. adnuit:** the subject is Apollo. **reducem:** Arruns. **ut videret:** the subject is **patria alta**; this clause, another substantive clause of purpose (or indir. command) corresponds to the second part of his prayer (i.e., the part not granted by Apollo).

798. **non dedit:** in contrast to **dedit** (795) and **adnuit** (797); ASYNDETON strengthens the contrast. **in ... Notos:** repeats the imagery of **volucres ... in auras** (795). **vocem:** i.e., of Arruns. **vertere:** alternate third pers. pl. perf.

799. **ut:** temporal; takes the indicative.

800. **convertere ... tulere:** alternate third pers. pl. perf. The entire line is a CHIASMUS.

801–2. **cuncti ... Volsci:** somehow the Volscians know that Camilla is about to be struck by Arruns' spear; this is in striking contrast to Camilla herself (**nihil ipsa**), who neither hears nor otherwise senses the approach of Arruns' fatal weapon. **nec aurae nec sonitus:** perhaps HENDIADYS, = **nec aurae sonitus. sonitus** may be similarly construed with **venientis ... teli,** i.e., as a HENDIADYS equivalent to **venientis teli sonitus.** Vergil's arrangement, however, is far more elegant to both eye and ear, and leads to far less confusion between and among genitives.

hasta sub exsertam donec perlata papillam
haesit virgineumque alte bibit acta cruorem.
805   Concurrunt trepidae comites dominamque ruentem
suscipiunt. Fugit ante omnes exterritus Arruns
laetitia mixtoque metu, nec iam amplius hastae
credere nec telis occurrere virginis audet.
Ac velut ille, prius quam tela inimica sequantur,

---

amplius *adv.* more, further
bibo, -ere, bibi drink
concurro, -ere, concurri, concursus hurry together, run together
cruor, cruoris, *m.* blood
domina, -ae, *f.* mistress, female leader
donec until
exsero, -ere, exserui, exsertus uncover, expose
exterreo, -ere, exterrui, exterritus scare, terrify
hasta, -ae, *f.* spear, javelin
inimicus, -a, -um hostile, unfriendly

laetitia, -ae, *f.* joy, happiness
occurro, -ere, occurri, occursus run to meet, hurry
papilla, -ae, *f.* breast, nipple
perfero, perferre, pertuli, perlatus carry, convey
prius quam (= **priusquam**) before, earlier than, sooner than
suscipio, -ere, suscepi, susceptus take from below, receive, take up
trepidus, -a, -um fearful, anxious
virgineus, -a, -um of a maiden, maidenly, virginal

---

803. The entire line exemplifies SYNCHYSIS, with the introductory conjunction **donec** delayed to the center of the line; the word order suggests Camilla's surprise and confusion at finding herself a target. **exsertam ... papillam**: the Amazons are traditionally described as baring a breast (or sometimes even removing it surgically) in order to make it easier to wield a bow and arrow; here, Camilla's bare breast suddenly becomes symbolic of her feminine vulnerability. **donec**: temporal (*until*) with indicative.

804. **haesit**: emphatic ENJAMBMENT as Arruns' weapon suddenly comes to a standstill in her body. **virgineum ... cruorem = virginis cruorem. alte**: construe either with the verb **bibit** or with the participle **acta**.

805–6. **trepidae comites**: the other Volscian warrior-maidens; now that Camilla's *aristeia* is over, they re-enter the scene. **ruentem suscipiunt**: they act quickly to catch her before she reaches the ground; cf. the

description of Dido at 4.391. **fugit**: the juxtaposition of sing. and pl. verbs emphasizes the isolation of Arruns, elaborated in the words **ante omnes**.

807–8. **laetitia mixtoque metu**: abl. abs.; the participle agrees with the second of the two nouns, but should be construed with both. **hastae**: dat. with **credere. credere ... occurrere**: complementary infs. with **audet. telis**: dat. with **occurrere**.

809. **ac velut**: the start of a SIMILE, in which Arruns is compared to a wolf hiding in the mountains after he has killed a shepherd or a bull. Vergil may well have chosen the subject of this SIMILE in part on the basis of a play on words since, according to Servius, the Sabine name for the priests of Apollo on Soracte, the Hirpi, is another word for *wolf* (**lupus**). **ille**: anticipates **lupus** in 811. **sequantur**: pres. subjunctive in a clause denoting an action anticipated rather than in process or completed.

continuo in montes sese avius abdidit altos   810
occiso pastore lupus magnove iuvenco,
conscius audacis facti, caudamque remulcens
subiecit pavitantem utero silvasque petivit:
haud secus ex oculis se turbidus abstulit Arruns
contentusque fuga mediis se immiscuit armis.   815

---

abdo, -ere, abdidi, abditus hide, conceal
audax, audacis daring, bold
avius, -a, -um pathless, out-of-the-way, remote
cauda, -ae, f. tail
conscius, -a, -um aware, conscious, guilty
contentus, -a, -um content, satisfied, happy
continuo *adv.* immediately, without delay
factum, -i, n. deed, action, act
immisceo, -ere, immiscui, immixtus mix in, mingle
iuvencus, -i, m. calf, young ox

lupus, -i, m. wolf
occido, -ere, occidi, occisus kill, slaughter
pastor, pastoris, m. shepherd
pavito (1) be afraid
remulceo, -ere, remulsi, remulsus smooth back, caress
secus *adv.* differently, otherwise
subicio, -ere, subieci, subiectus place beneath, put under
turbidus, -a, -um agitated, troubled, confused, in turmoil
uterus, -i, m. belly

---

810. **in montes ... altos**: recalls the mountaintop shrine of Apollo with which Arruns had associated himself in his prayer.

811. **occiso pastore ... magnove iuvenco**: abl. abs.; construe the participle with both **pastore** and **iuvenco. lupus**: the subject of the SIMILE is not identified until halfway through the third line; note its central position between the two abl. nouns.

812–13. **conscius audacis facti**: human awareness is attributed to the wolf. *Audacia* is an ambivalent concept in Roman thought: sometimes *boldness* in the best sense, sometimes *rashness* with a generally negative connotation. The behavior of the wolf as described in this couplet suggests that he himself is not sure which of these definitions applies. **caudam ... subiecit pavitantem utero**: the behavior of an animal fearing punishment, or cowering

before others. **utero**: dat. with compound verb. **silvas ... petivit**: the SIMILE concludes with a variation upon an image introduced earlier, **in montes ...avius ... altos** (810).

814. **haud secus**: the SIMILE concludes. **ex oculis**: i.e., of all the spectators. **turbidus**: ironically recalls Tarchon's rush into battle at 11.742.

815. **fuga**: abl. of specification or cause with **contentus**; repeats the emphasis on our last view of Arruns as craven (cf. **fugit** in 806). **mediis se immiscuit armis**: Arruns' departure from the narrative is open-ended; Vergil tells us nothing directly about what will become of him. Earlier in Book 11, however, Diana had told her nymph Opis that whoever killed Camilla would himself suffer a similar punishment (591–92).

816–35. The last words of Camilla and her death.

Illa manu moriens telum trahit, ossa sed inter
ferreus ad costas alto stat vulnere mucro.
Labitur exsanguis, labuntur frigida leto
lumina, purpureus quondam color ora reliquit.
820   Tum sic exspirans Accam ex aequalibus unam
adloquitur, fida ante alias quae sola Camillae
quicum partiri curas, atque haec ita fatur:
"Hactenus, Acca soror, potui: nunc vulnus acerbum
conficit, et tenebris nigrescunt omnia circum.

Acca, -ae, *f.* Acca, friend of Camilla

acerbus, -a, -um bitter, hostile, cruel

adloquor, adloqui, adlocutus address, speak to, console

aequalis, aequalis, *m.(f.)* age-mate, contemporary, equal

color, coloris, *m.* color

conficio, -ere, confeci, confectus complete, finish off, ruin, destroy

costa, -ae, *f.* rib

exsanguis, -e bloodless, pale

exspiro (1) breathe out, exhale

ferreus, -a, -um iron

frigidus, -a, -um cold, chill

hactenus *adv.* to this point, thus far

ita *adv.* thus, in such a way

mucro, mucronis, *m.* sword-point, sword

nigresco, -ere become black, grow dark

os, ossis, *n.* bone

partior, -iri, partitus share, divide up

purpureus, -a, -um reddish, purple; glowing, radiant

tenebrae, -arum, *f. pl.* darkness

---

816. **Illa**: the demonstrative draws our attention back to the dying Camilla. **ossa sed inter**: ANASTROPHE.

817. **ferreus … mucro**: the blade of Arruns' spear verbally surrounds Camilla, although physically her body surrounds it. **ad costas**: up against her ribs. **alto … vulnere**: abl. of place.

818–19. **labitur … labuntur**: ANAPHORA and ASYNDETON focus our attention on her slow but inexorable fall. **exsanguis**: not without blood, but losing it. **frigida … lumina**: cold is a symptom of death's proximity. The ENJAMBMENT of **lumina** fixes the viewer's attention on Camilla's eyes. **purpureus … color**: the pink tinge of the complexion of a person in good health; the color leaves her along with her blood. **quondam**: adv. modifying **purpureus**; her once-pink complexion is now drained of color.

820. **Accam**: one of Camilla's fellow Volscian warrior-maidens; named only in this

scene. **ex aequalibus**: partitive construction with **unam**; see note on 11.533.

821–22. Translate: **quae sola ante alias fida Camillae (fuit), (et) quicum partiri curas (solebat Camilla). Camillae**: dat. with **fida. quicum = quacum; qui** is an archaic form of the abl. rel. pronoun; the antecedent is Acca. **partiri**: either historical inf. or complementary to an implied verb such as **solebat**.

823. **hactenus … potui**: Camilla's final words are understated and brief; this might well be an inscription on a Roman funerary monument.

824. **conficit (me). tenebris**: abl. of description or specification. **nigrescunt**: Camilla's use of an inceptive verb form slows down the narrative, as Acca and we see Camilla deteriorate line by line. **omnia**: subject of **nigrescunt**. **circum**: either adverbial or prep. with **me** as an impled obj.

Effuge et haec Turno mandata novissima perfer: 825
succedat pugnae Troianosque arceat urbe.
Iamque vale." Simul his dictis linquebat habenas
ad terram non sponte fluens. Tum frigida toto
paulatim exsolvit se corpore, lentaque colla
et captum leto posuit caput, arma relinquens,   830
vitaque cum gemitu fugit indignata sub umbras.

---

arceo, -ere, arcui keep away, keep out

collum, -i, *n.* neck

effugio, -ere, effugi flee, run away

exsolvo, -ere, exsolvi, exsolutus unfasten, undo, set free, release

fluo, -ere, fluxi, fluctus flow, fall gradually

frigidus, -a, -um cold, chill

habena, -ae, *f.* rein, strap, cord

indignor, indignari, indignatus disdain, despise, resent

lentus, -a, -um supple, unyielding, pliant

linquo, -ere, liqui leave, let go

mandatum, -i, *n.* order, command, mandate

paulatim *adv.* little by little, gradually

perfero, perferre, pertuli, perlatus carry, bring, convey

spons, spontis, *f.* will, wish, desire

succedo, -ere, successi, successus advance, succeed, turn out well

valeo, -ere, valui be strong, fare well

---

825. **Turno**: dat. indir. obj. with **perfer**; in prose, **ad Turnum** would be more usual. **novissima**: most recent, i.e., last. Camilla's last thoughts concern military strategy and defense; her reference to Turnus here recalls the way the Camilla episode in Book 11 began, with a meeting between the two on the battlefield and his desire that she take charge of the battle on the plain (11.517–19). Now Camilla asks Acca to summon Turnus, since she herself will no longer be able to lead.

826. **succedat ... arceat**: pres. subjunctives; undertand either as jussive or as part of an indir. command following **mandata**, with **ut** omitted. **pugnae**: dat. with compound verb **succedat**. **urbe**: abl. of separation with **arceat**.

827. **simul**: prepositional here, taking as its abl. obj. **his dictis**.

828–30. **non sponte (sua)**. **fluens**: recalls the METAPHOR with which this episode began: see 11.501. **frigida**: in apposition to the

implied subject; note the repetition from 818. **toto ... corpore**: abl. of separation. **exsolvit**: **-v-** can be considered the vocalic **-u-** and so is a short syllable here; the preceding vowel (**-o-** in **-sol-**) is thus made short by position as well as by nature. **lenta ... colla et captum ... caput**: dir. obj. of **posuit**. **leto**: abl. of means with **captum**. Note how the sequence from **tum** to **caput** "flows" slowly from one line to the next, without any emphatic break; the description follows Camilla's slow decline and fall. **arma relinquens**: her last act in life is to give up her weapons.

831. **cum gemitu**: abl. of accompaniment. **indignata**: modifies **vita**. (Be careful not to translate this participle as its false cognate "indignant"—the point is rather that, as it descends to the underworld, Camilla's soul angrily laments its fate.) Precisely the same line closes the *Aeneid* (Book 12.952); Vergil uses it there to describe the death of Turnus.

Tum vero immensus surgens ferit aurea clamor
sidera: deiecta crudescit pugna Camilla;
incurrunt densi simul omnis copia Teucrum
835   Tyrrhenique duces Evandrique Arcades alae.

Arcas, Arcados, *m.* Arcadian, of Arcadia
copia, -ae, *f.* army, band
crudesco, -ere grow savage, become fierce
deicio, -ere, deieci, deiectus throw down,
cause to fall, strike, shoot down
densus, -a, -um dense, thick, close-packed
ferio, -ire strike, beat

immensus, -a, -um huge, boundless,
immeasurable
incurro, -ere, incurri, incursus rush,
charge at, run in
surgo, -ere, surrexi, surrectus rise,
emerge, extend upwards
vero *adv.* truly

832–33. **immensus ... clamor**: the silence
of the preceding scene is broken by the
crowd's reaction. **aurea ... sidera**: perhaps
ironic, as gold was the proximate cause
of Camilla's distraction; yet now it simply
describes the unchanging stars. **deiecta ...
Camilla**: abl. abs.

834. **Teucrum**: gen. pl.

Glossary of Rhetorical Terms and Figures of Speech Mentioned in the Notes

The following definitions are for the most part based on those found in Pharr's *Aeneid 1–6*. Note, however, that several terms are new to the list.

Alliteration is the repetition of the same letter or sound, usually at the beginning of a series of words, as at *Aen.* 11.698, *congeminat; vulnus calido rigat ora cerebro.* Alliteration is often used in combination with **onomatopoieia** (see below), as in this example.

Anacoluthon is a mid-sentence shift in syntax. The effect reflects the patterns of everyday speech. E.g., *Aen.* 11.552–54, where the syntax of *telum*, accusative in 552, shifts to dative (*huic*) in 554.

Analepsis is the description of events happening outside the narrative framework and before the time of the story of the *Aeneid* itself. E.g., the tale of Camilla's childhood and upbringing told by Diana to Opis at *Aen.* 11.535–94.

Anaphora is the repetition of a word or words at the beginning of successive clauses. E.g., *Aen.* 11.818–19, *Labitur exsanguis, labuntur frigida leto / lumina.* In Vergil, **anaphora** is often used in combination with **asyndeton** (see below), as in this example.

Anastrophe is the inversion of the normal order of words, as at *Aen.* 8.631, *ubera circum.*

Apostrophe is a sudden break from the previous narrative for an address, in the second person, to some person or object, absent or present. E.g., *Aen.* 8.643, *at tu dictis, Albane, maneres!*, addressed parenthetically to a character depicted on Aeneas' shield.

Asyndeton is the omission of conjunctions. E.g., *Aen.* 11.775–76, *sinus crepantes / carbaseos.*

Chiasmus is asymmetrical arrangement of four words or phrases in an *abBA* pattern; many combinations and variations are possible. E.g., *Aen.* 8.694, *Stuppea flamma manu telisque volatile ferrum.*

Ecphrasis is an extended and elaborate description of a work of art, a building, or a natural setting. E.g., *Aen.* 8.626–728, describing the scenes on the shield of Aeneas.

ENJAMBMENT is the continuation of a unit of thought beyond the end of one verse and into the first few feet of the next. E.g., *Aen.* 11.779–80, *captivo sive ut se ferret in auro / venatrix*, where *venatrix* emphasizes the significance of the hunting metaphor throughout the scene leading up to Camilla's death.

GOLDEN LINE is a term first used by the English poet Dryden to describe a five-word line consisting of two nouns and two adjectives symmetrically divided by a central verb (*abCAB* is the most recognizable pattern, although variation in the placement of nouns and adjectives is seen frequently). E.g., *Aen.* 8.684, *tempora navali fulgent rostrata corona.*

HENDIADYS is the expression of an idea by means of two nouns connected by a conjunction instead of by a noun and a modifying adjective, or by one noun modified by another. E.g., *Aen.* 11.539, *ob invidiam … viresque superbas = ob invidiam virium superbarum.*

HYSTERON PROTERON is the reversal of the natural or logical order of ideas. E.g., *Aen.* 11.676, *emissa manu contorsit spicula virgo*, where, contrary to logic, Camilla's spear is described as having been sent forth from her hand before she shoots it.

LITOTES is understatement, often enhanced by the use of the negative. E.g., *Aen.* 11.688, *Nomen … haud leve.*

METAPHOR is a very broad term for the use of a word or phrase appropriate to one area of imagery to describe something lying outside that area, and so to establish an implicit comparison. E.g., *Aen.* 11.501, *ad terram defluxit*, where a verb appropriate to the movement of water or a stream is applied to the movement of a character dismounting from a horse.

METONYMY is the substitution of one word for another which it suggests. E.g., *Aen.* 8.676, *instructo Marte*, where Mars represents the line of soldiers preparing to fight and thus war itself.

ONOMATOPOEIA is the use of words of which the sound suggests the sense. E.g., *Aen.* 11.698, *congeminat; vulnus calido rigat ora cerebro*, where the hard *c-* sound gruesomely echoes the sound made by Camilla's weapon as it strikes bone.

OXYMORON is the juxtaposition of two mutually contradictory words or phrases. E.g., *Aen.* 8.702, **scissa gaudens** *vadit Discordia palla.*

Pathetic fallacy is the attribution of human emotion to inanimate objects. E.g., *Aen*. 11.525, *aditusque maligni*, where Turnus' hideout is described as "ill-intentioned"; in fact it is Turnus' intention in hiding that is best described this way.

Personification is the attribution of human features, emotions, and/or other characteristics to abstract concepts or natural phenomena, e.g., *Discordia* at *Aen*. 8.702.

Polysyndeton is an overabundance of conjunctions, as at *Aen*. 11.675, *Tereaque Harpalycumque et Demophoonta Chromimque.*

Prolepsis is the description of events happening outside the narrative framework and after the time of the story of the *Aeneid* itself. E.g., all of the scenes depicted on the shield of Aeneas in Book 8.

Rhetorical question is a question that anticipates no real answer. E.g., *Aen*. 11.735 (Tarchon attempting to provoke his men's will to fight), *"Quo ferrum quidve haec gerimus tela inrita dextris?"*

Simile is a figure of speech that likens or asserts an explicit comparison between two different things. E.g., *Aen*. 8.621–23, *loricam ex aere rigentem, / sanguineam, ingentem, qualis cum caerula nubes / solis inardescit radiis longeque refulget.*

Synchysis is interlocking word order; many variations on the pattern *abAB* exist. E.g., *Aen*. 8.711, *magno maerentem corpore Nilum.*

Synecdoche is the use of a part for the whole, or the reverse. E.g., *Aen*. 11.690–91, *Orsilochum et Buten, duo maxima Teucrum / corpora*, where *corpora* is used of persons.

Synizesis is a metrical effect whereby two contiguous vowels within the same word and normally pronounced separately are slurred into one syllable. E.g. *Aen*. 11.768, *Chloreus*, where the last two vowels of the name are pronounced as one long vowel or diphthong.

Tmesis ("splitting") is the separation into two parts of a word normally written as one, often for a (quasi-)visual effect. E.g., *Aen*. 11.762, *Qua se cumque furens medio tulit agmine virgo*, where *qua + cumque = quacumque*; the word *se* is literally "surrounded" by the two parts of *quacumque*, and so places emphasis on Camilla as Arruns observes her.

Selected Bibliography

No bibliography of Vergil's *Aeneid* can hope to be complete or even comprehensive. I have focused, therefore, on recent work available in English and of particular relevance to the selections contained in this textbook. Most of the works cited are from the last two decades; exceptions are works of particular relevance and/or lasting impact. And of course, most are in English; but I have been unable to exclude a small number of works in Italian whose influence continues to be profound. While these are likely to be above and beyond the ability and interest of even the most avid student Vergilian, teachers with modest everyday Italian should be able to use these books and articles to their profit. Finally, I remind my readers to avail themselves of the Vergilian bibliography that appears in *Vergilius*, the annual publication of the Vergilian Society of America.

Texts and Commentaries

In composing this textbook, I have benefited from the labors of numerous predecessors, chief among whom are to be counted:

Fordyce, C. J., ed. *P. Vergili Maronis Aeneidos Libri VII–VIII*. Oxford, 1977.

Gransden, K. W., ed. *Virgil, Aeneid Book VIII*. Cambridge, 1976.

_____. *Virgil, Aeneid Book XI*. Cambridge, 1991.

Horsfall, N. M., ed. *Virgil Aeneid 11: A Commentary*. Leiden and Boston, 2003.

Traina, A., ed. *Virgilio: L'utopia e la storia (Il libro xii dell'Eneide e antologia delle opere)*. Turin, 1997.

Williams, R. D., ed. *The Aeneid of Virgil: Books 7–12*. Basingstoke and London, 1973; repr. 1984.

General Studies of and Collections of Essays on the AENEID

Anderson, W. S. *The Art of the Aeneid*. New York, 1969; repr. Wauconda, IL, 2005.

Anderson, W. S., and L. N. Quartarone, eds. *Approaches to Teaching Vergil's Aeneid*. New York, 2002.

Beye, Charles Rowan. *Ancient Epic Poetry: Homer, Apollonius, Virgil; With a Chapter on the Gilgamesh Poems*. Ithaca, NY, 1993; rev. and repr., Wauconda, IL, 2006.

Harrison, S. J., ed. *Oxford Readings in Vergil's Aeneid*. Oxford and New York, 1990.

Heinze, R. *Vergil's Epic Technique*, trans. H. and D. Harvey and F. Robertson. Bristol, 1993. (A valuable translation of the time-honored classic.)

Horsfall, N. *A Companion to the Study of Virgil*. Mnemosyne Supplement 151. Leiden and New York, 1995.

Martindale, C., ed. *The Cambridge Companion to Virgil*. Cambridge, 1997.

Perkell, C., ed. *Reading Vergil's Aeneid: An Interpretive Guide*. Norman, OK, 1999.

Quinn, S., ed. *Why Vergil? A Collection of Interpretations*. Wauconda, IL, 2000.

Harrison, Perkell, Quinn, Anderson-Quartarone, and Martindale are available in paperback, and should be on every Vergil teacher's shelf; Heinze and Horsfall should be within easy reach in the closest college or university library.

Works Focusing on the Passages in this Textbook

Bartsch, S. "*Ars* and the Man: The Politics of Art in Virgil's *Aeneid*." *Classical Philology* 93 (1998) 322–42.

Boyd, B. W. "Virgil's Camilla and the Traditions of Catalogue and Ecphrasis (*Aeneid* 7.803–17)." *American Journal of Philology* 113 (1992) 213–34.

_____. "*Non enarrabile textum*: Ecphrastic Trespass and Narrative Ambiguity in the *Aeneid*." *Vergilius* 41 (1995) 71–90.

Faber, R. "Vergil's *Shield of Aeneas* (*Aeneid* 8.617–731) and the *Shield of Heracles*." *Mnemosyne* 53 (2000) 48–57.

Fowler, D. "Vergil on Killing Virgins." In *Homo Viator: Classical Essays for John Bramble*, edited by M. Whitby, P. Hardie, and M. Whitby, 185–98. Bristol, 1987.

_____. "Deviant Focalisation in Virgil's *Aeneid*." *Proceedings of the Cambridge Philological Society* 36 (1990) 42–63.

_____. "Narrate and Describe: The Problem of Ekphrasis." *Journal of Roman Studies* 81 (1991) 25–35.

Kepple, L. R. "Arruns and the Death of Aeneas." *American Journal of Philology* 97 (1976) 344–60.

Miller, J. F. "Arruns, Ascanius, and the Virgilian Apollo." *Colby Quarterly* 30 (1994) 171–78.

Mitchell, R. "The Violence of Virginity in the *Aeneid*." *Arethusa* 24 (1991) 219–38.

Putnam, M. C. J. *Virgil's Epic Designs: Ekphrasis in the Aeneid.* New Haven, 1998.

Thomas, R. F. T. "Virgil's Ecphrastic Centerpieces." *Harvard Studies in Classical Philology* 87 (1983) 175–84.

Tissol, G. "An Allusion to Callimachus' *Aetia* 3 in Vergil's *Aeneid* 11." *Harvard Studies in Classical Philology* 94 (1992) 263–68.

West, G. S. "Chloreus and Camilla." *Vergilius* 31 (1985) 22–29.

Works for Further Reading and Research

a. on the *Aeneid*

Adler, E. *Vergil's Empire: Political Thought in the Aeneid.* Lanham, MD, 2003.

Barchiesi, A. *La traccia del modello: effetti omerici nella narrazione virgiliana.* Pisa, 1984.

Boyle, A. "The Canonic Text: Virgil's *Aeneid*." In *Roman Epic*, edited by A. Boyle, 79–107. London and New York, 1993.

Cairns, F. *Virgil's Augustan Epic.* Cambridge, 1989.

Clausen, W. *Virgil's Aeneid and the Tradition of Hellenistic Poetry.* Berkeley and Los Angeles, 1987.

_____. *Virgil's Aeneid: Decorum, Allusion, and Ideology.* Munich and Leipzig, 2002. (A revised reworking of the same author's earlier book [see above]; much new material is also included.)

Conte, G. B. *The Rhetoric of Imitation: Genre and Poetic Memory in Virgil and Other Latin Poets,* edited by C. P. Segal. Ithaca, NY, and London, 1986.

Corte, F. della, et al., eds. *Enciclopedia Virgiliana.* Six volumes. Rome, 1984–91.

Dyson, J. *King of the Wood: The Sacrificial Victor in Virgil's Aeneid.* Norman, OK, 2001.

Feeney, D. C. *The Gods in Epic.* Oxford, 1991.

Gillis, D. *Eros and Death in the Aeneid.* Rome, 1983.

Hardie, P. R. *Virgil's Aeneid: Cosmos and Imperium.* Oxford, 1986.

Horsfall, N. M. "The Aeneas Legend from Homer to Virgil." In *Roman Myth and Mythography,* by J. N. Bremmer and N. M. Horsfall, 12–24. BICS Suppl. 52. London, 1987.

Lyne, R. O. A. M. *Further Voices in Vergil's Aeneid.* Oxford, 1987.

_____. *Words and the Poet: Characteristic Techniques of Style in Vergil's Aeneid.* Oxford, 1989.

O'Hara, J. J. *Death and the Optimistic Prophecy in Vergil's Aeneid.* Princeton, 1990.

_____. *True Names: Vergil and the Alexandrian Tradition of Etymological Wordplay.* Ann Arbor, 1996.

Petrini, M. *The Child and the Hero: Coming of Age in Catullus and Vergil.* Ann Arbor, 1997.

Putnam, M. C. J. *Virgil's Aeneid: Interpretation and Influence.* Chapel Hill and London, 1995.

Rossi, A. *Contexts of War: Manipulation of Genre in Virgilian Battle Narrative.* Ann Arbor, 2003.

Stahl, H.-P., ed. *Vergil's Aeneid: Augustan Epic and Political Context*. London, 1997.

Syed, Y. *Vergil's Aeneid and the Roman Self. Subject and Nation in Literary Discourse*. Ann Arbor, 2004.

b. on the Augustan context

Galinsky, G. K. *Augustan Culture: An Interpretive Introduction*. Princeton, 1996.

———, ed. *The Cambridge Companion to the Age of Augustus*. Cambridge, 2005.

Gurval, R. *Actium and Augustus: The Politics and Emotions of Civil War*. Ann Arbor, 1995.

White, P. *Promised Verse: Poets in the Society of Augustan Rome*. Cambridge, MA, and London, 1993.

Zanker, P. *The Power of Images in the Age of Augustus*. Ann Arbor, 1988.

c. on the survival of Vergil

Martindale, C., ed. *Virgil and His Influence*. Bristol, 1984.

Thomas, R. F. T. *Virgil and the Augustan Reception*. Cambridge, 2001.

Wright, D. H. *The Vatican Vergil: A Masterpiece of Late Antique Art*. Princeton, 1993.

———. *The Roman Vergil and the Origins of Medieval Book Design*. Toronto, 2001.

Vocabulary

A

abdō, -ere, abdidī, abditus hide, conceal

abies, abietis, *f.* fir, object made of fir

aboleō, -ēre, abolēvī, abolitus destroy, wipe out

abundō (1) overflow, be abundant

Acca, -ae, *f.* Acca, friend of Camilla

accendō, -ere, accendī, accensum enflame, kindle, light

accingō, -ere, accinxī, accinctus gird oneself, prepare oneself

accipiter, accipitris, *m.* hawk

accommodus, -a, -um suitable for, convenient for

ācerbus, -a, -um bitter, hostile, cruel

acervus, -ī, *m.* heap, pile

aciēs, aciēī, *f.* a sharp edge; a line of vision; a battle line

Actius, -a, -um Actian, of or having to do with Actium

acus, -ūs, *f.* needle

acūtus, -a, -um pointed, sharp

addūcō, -ere, addūxī, adductus lead to, bring to; draw to the body

aditus, -ūs, *m.* approach, entrance, pass

adloquor, adloquī, adlocūtus address, speak to, console

adnuō, -ere, adnuī, adnūtus approve, nod approval, grant

adveniō, -īre, advēnī, adventus arrive at, come to

adventō (1) approach, draw near, arrive

adversus, -a, -um turned towards, facing, opposite, in front

Aegyptius, -a, -um Egyptian

Aegyptus, -ī, *f.* Egypt

Aeneadēs, -ae, *m.* companion or descendant of Aeneas, Trojan

aēnus, -a, -um of bronze, brazen

aequālis, aequālis, *m./f.* age-mate, contemporary, equal

aequus, -a, -um level, smooth, flat

aerātus, -a, -um decorated with bronze, brazen

aes, aeris, *n.* bronze

aestus, -ūs, *m.* tide, current, sea; heat

aeternus, -a, -um eternal, everlasting

aetherius, -a, -um ethereal, heavenly

aevum, -ī, *n.* age, span of time, lifetime

Āfer, Āfra, Āfrum African, of or having to do with Africa

agitō (1) stir up, set in motion, harass

agrestis, -e rustic, of the countryside, rural

Agrippa, -ae, *m.* M. Vipsanius Agrippa, friend and general of Augustus

āla, -ae, *f.* wing; band or troop of warriors, wing of an army

Albānus, -a, -um Alban, having to do with the town of Alba

albus, -a, -um white

āles, ālitis, *m./f.* large bird, bird of prey

aliter *adv.* otherwise, differently

almus, -a, -um nurturing, fostering, kindly

Alpīnus, -a, -um Alpine, having to do with the Alps

alternus, -a, -um one after the other, by turns

Amasēnus, -ī, *m.* Amasenus, a river of southern Latium

Amastrus, -ī, *m.* Amastrus, an ally of Aeneas

amnis, amnis, *m./ f.* river

amplexus, -ūs, *m.* embracing, caress, loving embrace

amplius *adv.* more, further

ancīle, ancīlis, *n.* figure-eight shield

anfractus, -ūs, *m.* bend, winding course, spiral

anguis, -is, *m.* snake, serpent

angustus, -a, -um narrow, thin, confined, tight

anser, anseris, *m.* goose

Antōnius, -ī, *m.* Marcus Antonius (often called Antony or Marc Antony in English)

Anūbis, -is, *m.* Anubis, Egyptian god with the body of a man and the head of a dog

apex, apicis, *m.* peak, top, cap

Apollō, Apollinis, *m.* Apollo, god of music, prophecy, archery and medicine

Appennīnicola, -ae, *m.* one who lives in the Appennines, Appennine-dweller

aquila, -ae, *f.* eagle

Arabs, Arabis, *m.* an Arab, inhabitant of Arabia

Araxēs, -is, *m.* Armenian river (modern name Aras)

Arcas, Arcados, *m.* Arcadian, of Arcadia

arceō, -ēre, arcuī keep away, keep out

arcus, -ūs, *m.* bow

ardor, ardōris, *m.* burning, fire, conflagration

argenteus, -a, -um silver, made from silver, silver-colored

argentum, -ī, *n.* silver

armentālis, -e having to do with herds, rustic

armō (1) arm, equip, furnish with weapons

arrigō, -ere, arrexī, arrectus stand up straight

arripiō, -ere, arripuī, arreptus snatch, seize, take possession of

Arruns, Arruntis, *m.* Arruns, an Etruscan

Ascanius, -ī, *m.* Ascanius, son of Aeneas

aspectus, -ūs, *m.* sight, glance, vision, view, gaze

astus, -ūs, *m.* cunning, craft, guile

attollō, -ere lift up, raise

audax, audācis daring, bold

Augustus, -ī, *m.* Augustus, honorific title assumed by Octavian in 27 BCE

Aunus, -ī, *m.* Aunus, a man from the mountains of northern Italy

aurātus, -a, -um ornamented with gold, gilded

Aurōra, -ae, *f.* the East, the Orient

āversus, -a, -um reversed, turned away from

āvius, -a, -um pathless, out-of-the-way, remote

āvolō (1) fly away, fly off

B

Bacchus, -ī, *m.* Bacchus, god of wine

Bactra, -ōrum, *n. pl.* the province of Bactra, in ancient Parthia

barbaricus, -a, -um barbarian, foreign

barbarus, -a, -um foreign

bellātor, bellātōris, *m.* fighter, warrior

Bellōna, -ae, *f.* Bellona, goddess of war

bibō, -ere, bibī drink

bicornis, -e two-horned

bivius, -a, -um crossable both ways, having two ways

bracchium, -ī, *n.* arm, branch

Būtēs, -is, *m.* Butes, an ally of Aeneas

C

caedēs, -is, *f.* slaughter, bloodshed, killing

caedō, -ere, cecīdī, caesus cut down, kill, slaughter

caelō (1) emboss, engrave, chisel

caerul(e)us, -a, -um blue, greenish blue; celestial

Caesar, Caesaris, *m.* Caesar, the *cognomen* used by members of one branch of the *gens Iulia*; after Augustus' reign, *Caesar* becomes an honorific title for all succeeding Roman emperors

caesariēs, -ēī, *f.* hair

caespes, caespitis, *m.* sod, turf, ground

calidus, -a, -um hot, warm, feverish

calx, calcis, *f.* heel

Camilla, -ae, *f.* Camilla, queen of the Volscians

candens, candentis shining, gleaming

candidus, -a, -um gleaming, dazzling white

cānus, -a, -um white, whitened

Capitōlium, -ī, *n.* the Capitoline hill, on which are located the citadel, the temple of Jupiter Optimus Maximus, and many other important temples and scenes of famous events in early Roman history

captīvus, -a, -um captured in war, captive

Cār, Cāris, *m.* Carian, inhabitant of Caria

carbaseus, -a, -um made of linen

Casmilla, -ae, *f.* Casmilla, mother of Camilla

cassida, -ae, *f.* helmet

castus, -a, -um chaste, upright, moral

caterva, -ae, *f.* band, crowd, throng, company, troops

Catilīna, -ae, *m.* L. Sergius Catilina, leader of a conspiracy against the Roman state during the consulship of Cicero

Catō, -ōnis, *m.* M. Porcius Cato, Roman consul and censor

cauda, -ae, *f.* tail

cavea, -ae, *f.* part of the theater where spectators sat, theater

cerebrum, -ī, *n.* brain, head, skull

cernō, -ere, crēvī, crētus distinguish, determine, perceive

cervīx, cervīcis, *f.* neck

cēterus, -a, -um the rest, the remaining

chlamys, chlamydis, *f.* cloak, cape

Chlōreus, -ī *or* -eī, *m.* Chloreus, an ally of Aeneas

chorus, -ī, *m.* chorus, troupe, group of people, group of worshippers

Chromis, -is, *m.* Chromis, an ally of Aeneas

Circensēs, -ium, *m. pl.* games held in the Circus Maximus

circu(m)eō, circu(m)īre, circu(m)iī, circu(m)itus go around, coil around, surround, encircle

circu(m)itus, -ūs, *m.* orbit, cycle, perimeter

circumdō, -are, circumdedī, circumdatus place around, surround, enclose

circumfundō, -ere, circumfūdī, circumfūsus pour around, surround

circumlīgō (1) bind, tie, fasten

citus, -a, -um quick, swift

claudō, -ere, clausī, clausus close, confine, enclose, envelop

clipeus, -ī, *m.* and **clipeum, -ī,** *n.* round shield

Cloelia, -ae, *f.* Cloelia, Roman girl who swam the Tiber to escape from Porsenna

Clytius, -ī, *m.* Clytius, a Trojan

Cocles, Coclitis, *m.* Horatius Cocles, a Roman who defended a bridge by himself in the war against Porsenna

cohors, cohortis, *f.* cohort, subdivision of a legion, armed force

colligō, -ere, collēgī, collectus gather together, gather, collect, pick up

collum, -ī, *n.* neck

color, colōris, *m.* color

columba, -ae, *f.* dove

comitor, comitārī, comitātus accompany, attend, escort

comminus *adv.* at close quarters, hand-to-hand

committō, -ere, commīsī, commissus bring together, expose to, entrust to

compellō (1) address, speak to

complector, complectī, complexus embrace, clasp, cling to

comprendō *or* **comprehendō, -ere, compr(eh)endī, compr(eh)ensus** take hold of, grip, hold

concieō, -ēre, concīvi, concitus stir up, excite

concipiō, -ere, concēpī, conceptus take, undertake, assume

concitō (1) set in motion, hurl, urge on, rouse, spur, stir

concurrō, -ere, concurrī, concursus hurry together, run together, charge

conferō, conferre, contulī, collatus carry, direct, engage

conficiō, -ere, confēcī, confectus complete, finish off, ruin, destroy

congeminō (1) double; use repeatedly, strike repeatedly

congredior, congredī, congressus meet, approach

coniunx, coniugis, *m./f.* partner, wife, husband, consort

cōnor, -ārī, cōnātus try, attempt

conscius, -a, -um aware, conscious, guilty

consequor, consequī, consecūtus pursue, overtake

conserō, -ere, conseruī, consertus connect, join, fasten together

consessus, -ūs, *m.* a sitting together, an assembly

consilium, -ī, *n.* plan, advice, decision, intention

consurgō, -ere, -surrexī, -surrectus rise, arise

contentus, -a, -um content, satisfied, happy

continuō *adv.* immediately, without delay

contorqueō, -ēre, contorsī, contortus twist, turn, agitate, send whirling, discharge

convellō, -ere, convellī, convulsus pull violently, batter, shatter

convertō, -ere, convertī, conversus rotate, reverse, turn backwards, turn, turn towards

convexus, -a, -um convex, rounded, vaulted, domed

copia, -ae, *f.* army, band

coquō, -ere, coxī, coctus harden by heat, bake, cook

cornū, cornūs, *n.* horn, ivory; bow

corōna, -ae, *f.* crown

corripiō, -ere, corripuī, correptus snatch, seize, take hold of

coruscō (1) brandish, wave, shake

costa, -ae, *f.* rib

crēdō, -ere, crēdidī, crēditus believe

crepō (1) rustle, crackle, rattle

crīnālis, -e worn in the hair

crista, -ae, *f.* crest of a helmet, plume

croceus, -a, -um saffron-colored, yellow

crūdescō, -ere grow savage, become fierce

cruentus, -a, -um bloody, bleeding, stained with blood

cruor, cruōris, *m.* blood

crūs, crūris, *n.* leg, shin

culmus, -ī, *m.* stalk, stem, thatch

cultor, cultōris, *m.* inhabitant, worshipper

cultrix, cultrīcis, *f.* female inhabitant, dweller

Cures, Curium, *m. pl.* Cures, chief town of the Sabines

curvus, -a, -um curved, winding, tortuous, twisting

cuspis, cuspidis, *f.* sharp point, spear, lance

Cybelus, -ī, *m.* Cybelus (or Cybele), a mountain in Phrygia sacred to the goddess Cybele

Cyclas, Cycladis, *f.* one of the Cyclades islands, near Delos

Cytherēa, -ae, *f.* Venus, goddess of Cythera, a Greek island close to which Venus was born from the foam of the sea

D

Dahae, -ārum, *m. pl.* the Dahae, a Scythian tribe

daps, dapis, *f.* feast, banquet

dēbeō, -ēre, dēbuī, debitus owe, ought

decus, decoris, *n.* honor, glory

dēdecus, dēdecoris, *n.* shame, dishonor, disgrace

dēfendō, -ere, dēfendī, defensus defend

dēfluō, -ere, dēfluxī, dēfluxus flow down, glide down, descend

dēfringō, -ere, dēfrēgī, dēfractum break off

dēiciō, -ere, dēiēcī, dēiectus throw down, cause to fall, strike, shoot down

dēlabor, dēlabī, dēlāpsus descend, glide down

delphin, delphīnis, *m.* dolphin

dēlūbrum, -ī, *n.* shrine, temple

Demophoon, -ntis, *m.* Demophoon, an ally of Aeneas

dens, dentis, *m.* tooth

densus, -a, -um dense, thick, close-packed

dēpendeō, -ēre, dēpendī hang down

dēprōmō, -ere, dēprompsī, dēpromptus fetch, take out, extract

dēripiō, -ere, dēripuī, dēreptus pull off, grab, snatch off

dēsiliō, -īre, dēsiluī jump down, dismount

dēsuper *adv.* from above

dētorqueō, -ēre, dētorsī, dētortus turn away, deflect, change direction

Diāna, -ae, *f.* Diana, virgin goddess of the hunt and the moon

differō, differre, distulī, dīlātus disperse, separate, draw or tear apart

dīmittō, -ere, dīmīsī, dīmissum send away, dismiss, put away

Dīrae, -ārum, *f. pl.* the Dirae, Italian goddesses associated with the Furies

Dīs, Ditis, *m.* Dis, ruler of the underworld; also known as Pluto(n)

discinctus, -a, -um ungirt, unbelted

Discordia, -ae, *f.* Discord, Disagreement

dispergō, -ere, dispersī, dispersus scatter, disperse

dīversus, -a, -um turned different ways, opposite, different

doleō, -ēre, doluī grieve, be in pain, feel grief, feel sorrow

domina, -ae, *f.* mistress, female leader

dōnec until

dorsum, -ī, *n.* back

dracō, dracōnis, *m.* snake

dubitō (1) be in doubt, hesitate

dubius, -a, -um uncertain, doubtful, unreliable

dulcēdō, dulcēdinis, *f.* sweetness, pleasantness

dūmus, -ī, *m.* thorn-bush, bramble

duo, duae, duo two

E

efferō, efferre, extulī, ēlātus carry away, lift

effor, effārī, effātus say, speak, utter

effugiō, -ere, effūgī flee, run away

effulgō, -ere, effulsī blaze forth, flash, gleam

ēgregius, -a, -um outstanding, pre-eminent, excellent

ēiciō, -ere, ēiēcī, ēiectus drive out, expel, cast out

ēlectrum, -ī, *n.* mixed metal (amber in color), electrum

ēlūdō, -ere, ēlūsī, ēlusus trick, deceive, escape, evade

ēminus *adv.* from a distance, from afar

ēmittō, -ere, ēmīsī, ēmissus send out, let loose, let fly, shoot

en behold! look!

ēnarrābilis, -e that can be described or explained, "describable"

equa, -ae, *f.* mare

eques, equitis, *m.* horseman, rider, knight; cavalry

Eunaeus, -ī, *m.* Eunaeus, an ally of Aeneas

Euphrātēs, -ī, *m.* Euphrates, river in Asia Minor

ēvādō, -ere, ēvāsī, ēvāsus escape, evade, go out of

ēventus, -ūs, *m.* outcome, result

ēviscerō (1) disembowel, eviscerate

excēdō, -ere, excessī, excessus go away, depart, leave

excipiō, -ere, excēpī, exceptus take, take up

exemplum, -ī, *n.* example

exeō, exīre, exiī *or* **exīvī, exitus** go out; elude, escape

exigō, -ere, exēgī, exactus drive out; extend, undergo, spend (time)

expleō, -ēre, explēvī, explētus fill, appease, satisfy

explōrātor, explōrātōris, *m.* scout, spy

exsanguis, -e bloodless, pale

exserō, -ere, exseruī, exsertus uncover, expose

exsilium, -ī, *n.* banishment, exile

exsolvō, -ere, exsolvī, exsolūtus unfasten, undo, set free, release

exspectō (1) wait for, expect, look forward to

exspīrō (1) breathe out, exhale

exsultō (1) jump, leap

exsurgō, -ere, exsurrexī rise up, stand up

exterreō, -ēre, exterruī, exterritus scare, terrify

extundō, -ere, extudī, extūsus hammer, produce with effort, emboss

exuviae, -ārum, *f. pl.* armor, spoils; skin stripped from dead beast

F

facile *adv.* easily

facilis, -e easy, straightforward

factum, -ī, *n.* deed, action, act

fallax, fallācis deceitful, lying

famula, -ae, *f.* serving woman, maid, attendant

fātifer, -era, -erum death-dealing, deadly, destructive

fatīgō (1) tire out, exhaust; assail, harass

faucēs, -ium, *f. pl.* throat; entrance, pass, passage

fēmina, -ae, *f.* woman

femineus, -a, -um womanly, belonging to a woman, woman's

fera, -ae, *f.* wild beast

ferīnus, -a, -um wild, belonging to wild beasts

feriō, -īre strike, beat

feritās, feritātis, *f.* savagery, fierceness, ferocity

ferrātus, -a, -um iron covered, armored

ferreus, -a, -um iron

ferrūgō, ferrūginis, *f.* rust, rust-colored

ferveō, -ere, fervī boil

fētus, -a, -um pregnant

fīdō, -ere, —, fīsus trust, have confidence in, rely on

fīdūcia, -ae, *f.* assurance, confidence, reliance, trust

fīlius, -ī, *m.* son

fingō, -ere, finxī, fictus stroke, form, shape

flagellum, -ī, *n.* whip, lash

fluō, -ere, fluxī, fluctus flow, fall gradually

fluvius, -ī, *m.* river, stream

foedus, foederis, *n.* treaty, league, compact

forte *adv.* by chance, accidentally, fortuitously

fraus, fraudis, *f.* mischief, deceit, guile; harm, danger

fremō, -ere, fremuī, fremitus roar, rumble

frēnum, -ī, *n.* rein, bridle

frētus, -a, -um relying on, confident in

frīgidus, -a, -um cold, chill

frons, frondis, *f.* foliage, leafy bough

frustrā *adv.* in vain, uselessly

fugax, fugācis evasive, fleeting, fleeing

fulgeō, -ēre, fulsī, fulsus gleam, shine, glitter

fulvus, -a, -um tawny

funda, -ae, *f.* sling (for hurling stones)

fūnis, -is, *m.* rope, cable

Furiae, -ārum, *f. pl.* the Furies, goddesses of vengeance

furtim *adv.* secretly, furtively

furtum, -ī, *n.* theft; secret, deception; stratagem

G

gaesum, -ī, *n.* long, heavy javelin of the Gauls

galea, -ae, *f.* helmet

Gallus, -ī, *m.* a Gaul

gaudeō, -ēre, gāvīsus sum rejoice, delight, take pleasure in

Gelōnī, -ōrum, *m. pl.* Geloni, a people of Scythia

glōria, -ae, *f.* glory

Gortȳnius, -a, -um of or belonging to Gortynia, Gortynian, Cretan

gradior, gradī, gressus step, walk, proceed

grāmineus, -a, -um grassy

grandis, -e great, large

grātēs, -ium, *f. pl.* thanks, thanksgiving

gremium, -ī, *n.* lap, bosom

grūs, gruis, *f.* crane, large bird

gȳrus, -ī, *m.* circle, circling movement, ring

H

habēna, -ae, *f.* rein, strap, cord

habilis, -e easy to handle, easily fitted

habitus, -ūs, *m.* style, fashion, custom

hāctenus *adv.* to this point, thus far

Harpalycus, -ī, *m.* Harpalycus, an ally of Aeneas

haruspex, haruspicis, *m.* diviner, interpreter of omens

hasta, -ae, *f.* spear, javelin

hastīle, hastīlis, *n.* spear, handle of a spear

hiātus, -ūs, *m.* opening, yawning, gaping

Hippotadēs, -ae, *m.* descendant/son of Hippotes

horrendus, -a, -um terrible, awe-inspiring, venerable

hostia, -ae, *f.* sacrificial animal, sacrificial victim

humus, -ī, *f.* ground, earth, soil

I

iaculum, -ī, *n.* javelin

Iāpyx, Iāpygis Iapygian, from or belonging to southern Italy; (used as a noun) *m.* Iapyx, the northwest wind

ignāvia, -ae, *f.* sloth, lack of spirit

igneus, -a, -um burning, fiery, ardent

ignipotens, -ntis potent in fire, ruler of fire, powerful in fire

ignōtus, -a, -um unfamiliar, unknown

illīc *adv.* there, yonder

imber, imbris, *m.* rain, shower, rainstorm

imitor, -ārī, imitātus imitate, copy, follow

immensus, -a, -um huge, boundless, immeasurable

immisceō, -ēre, immiscuī, immixtus mix in, mingle

immittō, -ere, immīsī, immissus send, throw, release, let loose

immortālis, -e immortal, undying

immulgeō, -ēre milk

impavidus, -a, -um fearless, undaunted

implicō, -āre, implicuī, implicātus enfold, wrap inside, entwine

improbus, -a, -um unprincipled, shameless, presumptuous, wicked

inardescō, -ere, inarsī burn, glow, gleam

incautus, -a, -um not cautious, careless

incēdō, -ere, incessī proceed, walk, step

incidō, -ere, incidī, incāsus fall upon, chance to meet, come across

incito (1) set in motion, provoke, rouse

incolumis, -e safe, unharmed

incumbō, -ere, incubuī lean forward; apply oneself with energy

incurrō, -ere, incurrī, incursus rush, charge at, run in

indīcō, -ere, indīxī, indictum announce, proclaim

indignor, -ārī, indignātus disdain, despise, resent, be angry, be indignant, complain, protest

indomitus, -a, -um wild, fierce, untamed

Indus, -ī, m. inhabitant of India

inermis, -e unarmed

iners, inertis lazy, inactive, spiritless

infans, infantis, m./f. baby, infant

infaustus, -a, -um ill-starred, unlucky, cursed

inferō, inferre, intulī, illātus carry in, bring, impel

inglōrius, -a, -um undistinguished, unhonored

ingredior, ingredī, ingressus enter upon, go into, start

inimīcus, -a, -um hostile, unfriendly

inīquus, -a, -um uneven, unfair, rough, treacherous

innectō, -ere, innexuī, innexum fasten, garland, surround

innō (1) swim in, swim

inritus, -a, -um unfulfilled, ineffectual, bringing no result

inscius, -a, -um not knowing, ignorant

insideō, -ēre, insēdī, insessus sit in, lie in ambush, rest upon

insidiae, -ārum, f. pl. ambush, surprise attack, plot

insignis, -e notable, distinguished

insonō, -āre, insonuī make a sound, resound

inspoliātus, -a, -um not plundered, not despoiled

instīgō (1) incite, impel, urge on, stir up

instō, -āre, institī stand on; assail, press, urge on

instruō, -ere, instruxī, instructus construct, draw up (in a battle formation)

insurgō, -ere, insurrexī rise, extend up

intemerātus, -a, -um undefiled, pure, inviolate

interior, interius inner, internal, inside of

interritus, -a, -um fearless, not terrified

invehō, -ere, invexī, invectus carry in(to), bring in(to)

invidia, -ae, f. ill will, envy, jealousy

invīsō, -ere, invīsī, invīsus go to see, visit

iste, ista, istud that, that of yours

ita *adv.* thus, in such a way, in this way

Italia, -ae, f. Italy

Italus, -a, -um Italian, having to do with Italy

iugulum, -ī, n. neck, throat

iungō, -ere, iunxī, iunctus join, unite

iūs, iūris, n. law

iuvencus, -ī, m. bull, young ox, calf, cattle

L

labrum, -ī, *n.* lip

lac, lactis, *n.* milk

lacertus, -ī, *m.* and **lacertum, -ī,** *n.* arm, upper arm

lacessō, -ere, lacessīvī (*or* **-iī**), **lacessītus** challenge, provoke, arouse

lacteus, -a, -um milky, milk-white

laetitia, -ae, *f.* happiness, joy

laevus, -a, -um left, left-handed

lambō, -ere, lambī lick

lāniger, lānigera, lānigerum wool-bearing, fleecy

lātē *adv.* far and wide, broadly

latebrōsus, -a, -um hidden, secret

Latīnus, -a, -um Latin, belonging to Latium

Lātōnius, -a, -um of or having to do with Leto (Latona), mother of Apollo and Diana

lātrātor, lātrātōris, *m.* barker, one who barks

Laurentēs, -um, *m. pl.* the Laurentines (inhabitants of Laurentum, a sea town in Latium)

laxus, -a, -um loose, slack

Leleges, -um, *m. pl.* Lelegians, early inhabitants of the coast of Asia Minor

lentus, -a, -um supple, unyielding, pliant

lētālis, -e deadly, lethal

Leucātē, -ēs, *f.* promontory on southern side of the island of Leucas

levis, -e light, light-weight, trivial

lēvis, -e smooth

liber, librī, *m.* inner bark of a tree, bark

lībertās, lībertātis, *f.* freedom, liberty

lībrō (1) level, balance, aim

Ligus, -uris, *m.* a Ligurian, an inhabitant of Cisalpine Gaul

lingua, -ae, *f.* tongue; language

linquō, -ere, līquī leave, let go

Līris, Līris, *m.* Liris, an ally of Aeneas

longē *adv.* a long way off, from afar

lōrīca, -ae, *f.* leather cuirass, breastplate

lūbricus, -a, -um slippery, inconstant

lūceō, -ēre, luxī be bright, shine, gleam, glitter

luctor, luctārī, luctātus wrestle, struggle

lūdō, -ere, lūsī, lūsus play

lūdus, -ī, *m.* game, sport

lupa, -ae, *f.* she-wolf

Lupercus, -ī, *m.* priest of Lycaean Pan

lupus, -ī, *m.* wolf

lustra, -ōrum, *n. pl.* wilds, lairs

Lycius, -a, -um of or belonging to Lycia, Lycian

M

Maeonidae, -ārum, *m. pl.* Etruscans

maereō, -ēre mourn, grieve

māla, -ae, *f.* jaw(s)

malignus, -a, -um ungenerous, scanty, spiteful, unkind

mamma, -ae, *f.* teat, udder

mandātum, -ī, *n.* order, command, mandate

mandō, -ere, mandī, mansus chew, bite, crush with teeth

mānēs, -ium, *m. pl.* (souls of) the dead, Hades

Manlius, -ī, *m.* M. Manlius Capitolinus, who alerted Rome to the invasion of the Gauls

Mars, Martis, *m.* Mars, god of war

Māvors, Māvortis, *m.* Mars, god of war

memor, memoris mindful, aware, remembering

mendax, mendācis given to lying, mendacious, deceptive, lying

meritō *adv.* deservedly, justly

Messāpus, -ī, *m.* Messapus, an Italian leader

Metabus, -ī, *m.* Metabus, one-time ruler of Privernum

Mettus, -ī, *m.* Mett(i)us Fufetius, an Alban general

mīles, mīlitis, *m.* soldier, soldiery, troops

mīlitia, -ae, *f.* military service

minax, minacis threatening, menacing

Minerva, -ae, *f.* Minerva, goddess of wisdom and the arts

minor, -ari, minatus threaten, menace

minus *adv.* less, fewer, to a smaller extent

miror, -ari, miratus be amazed, marvel at

miserandus, -a, -um pitiable, poor

mōlēs, -is, *f.* great mass, pile

mollis, -e gentle, soft, mild, tender

Morīnī, -ōrum, *m. pl.* Morini, a tribe from Belgium

morior, morī, mortuus die

mox *adv.* soon

mucrō, mucrōnis, *m.* sword-point, sword

mulceō, -ēre, mulsī, mulsus touch lightly, caress, soothe

Mulciber, Mulciberī, *m.* epithet for Vulcan, perhaps alluding to his ability to polish and smoothe (> **mollīre**) the metalwork he crafts

muliebris, -e of or belonging to a woman, womanly, feminine, effeminate

N

nāta, -ae, *f.* daughter, young girl

nāvālis, -e naval, nautical

necdum and not yet

nefās *n. (indecl.)* crime (lit., unspeakable thing)

Neptūnius, -a, -um of or having to do with Neptune

Neptūnus, -ī, *m.* Neptune, god of the sea

nequeō, -īre, nequīvī, nequitus be unable, cannot

nēquīquam *adv.* in vain, uselessly

niger, nigra, nigrum black, dark

nigrescō, -ere become black or dark

nihil, *n. (indecl.)* nothing, not, not at all

Nīlus, -ī, *m.* Nile river

niveus, -a, -um snow-white, snowy

nocturnus, -a, -um nocturnal, belonging to the night

nōdus, -ī, *m.* knot

Nomades, -um, *m. pl.* Nomads, a wandering tribe

nōtus, -a, -um known

Notus, -ī, *m.* Notus, the south wind

nūbes, -is, *f.* cloud

nūdus, -a, -um naked, bare, exposed

numquam *adv.* never

nuntiō (1) announce, report

nurus, -ūs, *f.* daughter-in-law

nutriō, -īre, nutrīvī, nutrītus nourish, feed

nympha, -ae, *f.* nymph

O

observō (1) observe, take notice of, watch

obsidiō, obsidiōnis, *f.* siege, blockade

obsīdō, -ere besiege, occupy, take possession of

obuncus, -a, -um hooked, curved

obvius, -a, -um meeting, so as to meet, to meet

occīdō, -ere, occīdī, occīsus kill, slaughter

occurrō, -ere, occurrī, occursus run to meet, hurry

ocrea, -ae, *f.* greave

offerō, offerre, obtulī, oblātus present, offer, bring before

ōlim *adv.* formerly, once

olor, olōris, *m.* swan

Olympus, -ī, *m.* Olympus, home of the gods

omnigenus, -a, -um of every kind

omnipotens, omnipotentis all powerful, omnipotent

onus, oneris, *n.* burden, load

opācus, -a, -um dark

operiō, -īre, operuī, opertus close, cover, shroud

Opis (*or* **Ops), Opis,** *f.* Opis, a nymph

oppidum, -ī, *n.* town

Oriens, Orientis, *m.* the Orient

Ornytus, -ī, *m.* Ornytus, an ally of Aeneas

Orsilochus, -ī, *m.* Orsilochus, an ally of Aeneas

os, ossis, *n.* bone

ostium, -ī, *n.* door, entrance

ostrum, -ī, *n.* purple color, purple

ovō (1) rejoice, exult

P

Pagasus, -ī, *m.* Pagasus, an ally of Aeneas

palla, -ae, *f.* cloak, mantle, garment, robe

pallens, pallentis pale, pallid

palma, -ae, *f.* palm, hand

pālor, pālārī, pālātus wander, scatter, stray

papilla, -ae, *f.* breast, nipple

pariter *adv.* equally, evenly, likewise, together

parma, -ae, *f.* shield

partior, -īrī, partītus share, divide up

parvus, -a, -um small, little

pascor, pascī, pastus feed, pasture, nourish

pastor, pastōris, *m.* shepherd

pater, patris, *m.* father; senator

patria, -ae, *f.* country, homeland

paulatim *adv.* little by little, gradually

pavitō (1) be afraid

pedes, peditis, *m.* foot-soldier, infantryman

pedester, pedestris, pedestre pedestrian, on foot

pellis, -is, *f.* skin, hide

pellō, -ere, pepulī, pulsus strike, beat, drive, impel

Penātēs, -ium, *m. pl.* gods of the household and of the Roman state

pendeō, -ēre, pependī (intrans.) *or* **pendō, -ere, pependī, pensus** (trans.) hang; hang from, hang around

penna, -ae, *f.* wing

peregrīnus, -a, -um foreign

pererrō (1) wander through, traverse, meander

perferō, perferre, pertulī, perlātus carry, bring, convey

perficiō, -ere, perfēcī, perfectum complete, finish, carry out

pergō, -ere, perrexī, perrectus proceed, go on

perīculum, -ī, *n.* danger, trial

pernix, pernīcis swift, speedy

pestis, pestis, *f.* plague, curse, pest

pharetra, -ae, *f.* quiver

Phoebus, -ī, *m.* another name for Apollo

Phrygius, -a, -um Phrygian, Trojan

pīlentum, -ī, *n.* easy chariot or carriage

pīneus, -a, -um of pine, made of pine-wood

pingō, -ere, pinxī, pinctus paint, decorate, adorn, embroider

pinguis, -e rich, fat, fertile, plump

plānitiēs, -ēī, *f.* level surface, flat space, plateau

planta, -ae, *f.* sole (of the foot); tread, walking, step

plausus, -ūs, *m.* applause, approval

plēnus, -a, -um full

plūma, -ae, *f.* feather

pōculum, -ī, *n.* cup

polus, -ī, *m.* sky, heaven

pons, pontis, *m.* bridge

porca, -ae, *f.* pig, sow

Porsenna, -ae, *m.* Lars Porsenna, a king of Etruria who made war on Rome

porticus, -ūs, *f.* colonnade, porch, portico

portō (1) carry

poscō, -ere, poposcī demand, request; call, summon

postis, -is, *m.* door-post

postrēmus, -a, -um last, final

prae (+*abl.*) in front of, before

praeda, -ae, *f.* booty, spoils, prize

praefīgō, -ere, praefīxī, praefīxus attach, fasten

praemittō, -ere, praemīsī, praemissus send ahead

prehendō, -ere, prehendī, prehensus grasp, sieze, take hold of

prius quam (= **priusquam**) before, earlier than, sooner than

Prīvernum, -ī, *n.* Privernum, a Latin town, chief town of the Volscians

procella, -ae, *f.* blast, storm, storm-wind

prōcumbō, -ere, prōcubuī, prōcubitus bend forward, lie down

proelium, -ī, *n.* battle, conflict

prōmittō, -ere, prōmīsī, prōmissus send forth, let loose; promise; foretell

propius *adv.* nearer, more closely

prōtegō, -ere, prōtēxī, prōtectus cover, protect

prōtinus *adv.* straightaway, immediately

prūna, -ae, *f.* live coal, hot ash

puerīlis, -e of a child, belonging to a child

pugnātor, pugnātōris, *m.* fighter, warrior

pugnō (1) fight, combat

purpureus, -a, -um reddish, purple; glowing, radiant

pūrus, -a, -um clean, pure, free of decoration, unadorned, plain

putō (1) think, suppose

Q

quācumque *adv.* by whatever way, wherever

quadrīgae, -ārum, *f. pl.* team of four, four-horsed chariot

quadripes, quadripedis (or **quadru-**) four-footed; (*used as noun*) *m.* a four-footed animal

quālis, -e such (as)

quandō when, since, as

quandōquidem since, seeing that

quatiō, -ere, —, quassus shake, disturb, cause to tremble, brandish

quercus, -ūs, *f.* oak, oaktree

quia because, since

quisque, quaeque, quidque (quodque) each, every one

quot how many?; as many as

R

radians, -ntis beaming, shining, gleaming

radius, -ī, *m.* beam, ray

rapidus, -a, -um swift, rapid

raptō (1) snatch up, seize and carry off, plunder, lay waste, drag

recēns, recentis fresh, new, recent

receptus, -ūs, *m.* retreat, shelter, refuge

recognoscō, -ere, recognōvī, recognitus acknowledge, give recognition to

recoquō, -ere, recoxī, recoctus cook again, reforge

redarguō, -ere, redarguī prove untrue, refute, disprove

redeō, redīre, rediī *or* **redīvī, reditus** return, go back

redūcō, -ere, reduxī, reductus lead back, draw back

reductus, -a, -um drawn back, remote, distant

redux, reducis returning, coming home

reficiō, -ere, refēcī, refectus repair, restore, renew

reflectō, -ere, reflēxī, reflēctus bend back, turn back

refulgeō, -ēre, refulsī flash back, reflect, shine bright, glitter

rēgia, -ae, *f.* royal palace, residence

regiō, regiōnis, *f.* area, direction, region, line

remeō (1) return, go back

remulceō, -ēre, remulsī, remulsus smooth back, caress

reportō (1) carry back, bring back, take back, report

repugnō (1) fight back, defend, offer resistance

resistō, -ere, restitī resist, stop, pause, stand firm

revellō, -ere, revellī, revulsus tear loose, tear up

revolvō, -ere, revolvī, revolūtus roll back, wind up, turn over

Rhēnus, -ī *m.* Rhine river

rigeō, -ēre be stiff

rigō (1) make wet, soak, drench

rīmor, rīmārī, rīmātus search out, examine, scrutinize

rīpa, -ae, *f.* bank (of a river)

rīvus, ī, *m.* stream, brook

Rōma, -ae, *f.* Rome

Rōmānus, -a, -um Roman, having to do with Rome

Rōmuleus, -a, -um of or belonging to Romulus

Rōmulidae, -ārum, *m. pl.* the descendants of Romulus, the Romans

rōrō (1) let fall, drop, trickle, be dewy

rostrātus, -a, -um beaked

rostrum, -ī, *n.* beak of a ship

ruber, rubra, rubrum red, reddish

rubescō, -ere, rubuī become red, redden

S

Sabaeus, -a, -um Sabaean, of or from Arabia

Sābīnus, -a, -um Sabine, having to do with the Sabines, an ancient Italian people adjoining the Latins

saeviō, -īre, saeviī rage, act savagely

sagitta, -ae, *f.* arrow

sagittifer, -era, -erum arrow-carrying

sagulum, -ī, *n.* military cloak

Saliī, -ōrum, *m. pl.* Salii, priests dedicated to the service of Mars

sanctus, -a, -um sacred, holy, inviolate

sanguineus, -a, -um bloody, of blood, blood-red

sator, satōris, *m.* sower, begetter, progenitor

saucius, -a, -um wounded

scelus, sceleris, *n.* crime

scindō, -ere, scicidī *or* **scidī, scissus** tear, rend

scūtum, -ī, *n.* shield

sēcernō, -ere, sēcrēvī, sēcrētus separate, cut off

secō, -āre, secuī, sectum cut, divide

sēcrētus, -a, -um existing apart, separate from, set apart

secūris, -is, *f.* axe, hatchet

secus *adv.* differently, otherwise

segnis, -e lazy, slothful, sluggish

semita, -ae, *f.* path, track

semper *adv.* always

senex, senis old, aged

sententia, -ae, *f.* idea, opinion, belief, decision

serpens, serpentis, *m./f.* snake, serpent

seu, sīve either. . . or; whether. . . or

sevērus, -a, -um strict, austere, stern

sībilō (1) hiss

silvestris, -e woodland, belonging to woods

singulī, -ae, -a separate, individual, single

sinō, -ere, sīvī, situs leave, let, allow, permit

sinuōsus, -a, -um bending, curving, twisting

sinus, -ūs, *m.* fold (of a garment), hollow, curve; bosom; embrace

sistrum, -ī, *n.* rattle, used in worship of Isis

sīve, seu either. . . or; whether. . . or

solidus, -a, -um solid, firm, strong

solum, -ī, *n.* soil, earth, floor

Sōracte, -is, *n.* Soracte, a mountain in Etruria

sparus, -ī, *m.* hunting spear

specula, -ae, *f.* lookout, watch-tower, height

spīculum, -ī, *n.* point of a weapon, arrow

spolium, -ī, *n.* spoils, booty

spons, spontis, *f.* will, wish, desire

squāma, -ae, *f.* scale

sternō, -ere, strāvī, strātum lay down, stretch out on the ground, lay low

stimulus, -ī, *m.* goad, prick, spur, provocation

stirps, stirpis, *f.* offspring, descendant

strīdeō, -ēre and **strīdō, -ere, strīdī** hiss, whirr, whistle, make a high-pitched sound

Strȳmonius, -a, -um belonging to the river Strymon, Strymonian

studium, -ī, *n.* inclination, zeal, pursuit, desire

stuppeus, -a, -um made of tow, hempen

sūber, sūberis, *n.* cork-oak, cork

sūbiciō, -ere, sūbiēcī, sūbiectus place beneath, put under

subitō *adv.* suddenly, unexpectedly

subitus, -a, -um sudden, unexpected

sublīmis, -e high, elevated, aloft

subsistō, -ere, substitī stand firm, stay in place

succēdō, -ere, successī, successus advance, succeed, turn out well

suffundō, -ere, suffūdī, suffūsus pour on; spread beneath, stretch beneath

sūmō, -ere, sumpsī, sumptus take up, take possession of; (+ **poenās**) exact (a penalty)

suprā (+*acc.*) on top of, above; (*adv.*) on top, higher

surgō, -ere, surrexī, surrectus rise, emerge, extend upwards

suscipiō, -ere, suscēpī, susceptus take from below, receive, take up

suscitō (1) stir, rouse, arouse

suspendō, -ere, suspendī, suspensus hang, hang up

sustineō, -ēre, sustinuī lift, support; check, withstand; keep from

T

tacitus, -a, -um silent

Tarchon, Tarchōnis, *m.* Tarchon, Etruscan leader, ally of Aeneas

tardō (1) check, slow down, hold back

Tarpēius, -a, -um Tarpeian, a member of the *gens Tarpeia* or an epithet associated with one part of the Capitolium

Tarquinius, -ī, *m.* Tarquinius Superbus, last king of Rome

Tartareus, -a, -um Tartarean, of or having to do with the underworld

Tatius, ī, *m.* Titus Tatius, a king of the Sabines

tegmen, tegminis, *n.* covering

tegō, -ere, texī, tectus cover

tempus, temporis, *n.* side of the forehead, temple

tenebrae, -ārum, *f. pl.* darkness, shadow, darkness of night

tener, tenera, tenerum tender, delicate, of tender age

tenuis, -e slender, narrow, thin

teres, teretis smooth

Tēreus, -eī *or* **-eos,** *m.* Tereus, an ally of Aeneas

terreō, -ēre, terruī, territus fill with fear, terrify, alarm

terribilis, -e dreadful, terrible, terrifying

terror, terrōris, *m.* fear, terror; person or thing that creates terror

testor, testārī, testātus call to witness, appeal to

textum, -ī, *n.* that which is fitted together, structure, texture

tībia, -ae, *f.* pipe, reed instrument

Tīburs, Tīburtis belonging to Tibur; inhabitant of Tibur

Tīburtus, -ī, *m.* Tiburtus, a founder of Tibur

tigris, tigridis, *f.* tiger

timeō, -ēre, timuī fear, be afraid, fear for

trādō, -ere, trādidī, trāditus hand over, hand down

trāiciō, -ere, trāiēcī, trāiectus throw across, pierce, transfix

trāmes, trāmitis, *m.* footpath, path

transeō, -īre, transiī *or* **transīvī, transitus** go across, go past, pass

transverberō (1) transfix, pierce through

trepidus, -a, -um fearful, anxious

tridens, tridentis having three prongs

triplex, triplicis threefold, triple

triumphus, -ī, *m.* triumph, triumphal procession

Trīvia, -ae, *f.* Trivia, another name for Diana

tropaeum, -ī, *n.* trophy, victory

Trōs, Trōis, *m.* Tros, the name of a Trojan (grandson of Dardanus)

Tullus, -ī, *m.* Tullus Hostilius, third king of Rome

tumidus, -a, -um swollen

tunica, -ae, *f.* tunic

turbidus, -a, -um agitated, troubled, confused, in turmoil

turbō (1) agitate, disturb, confuse, upset

turbō, turbinis, *m.* whirlwind

turma, -ae, *f.* squadron, company

Turnus, -ī, *m.* Turnus, leader of the Rutulians and opponent of Aeneas

turrītus, -a, -um turreted, having towers

tūtus, -a, -um protected, safe, secure

Tyrrhēnus, -a, -um Etruscan, Tyrrhenian

U

ūber, ūberis, *n.* teat, udder, breast

ultimus, -a, -um farthest, most distant

ultrix, ultrīcis, *f.* avenger, avenging

ultrō *adv.* of one's own accord, voluntarily

uncus, -a, -um curved, hooked

unguis, -is, *m.* claw, talon

urgeō, -ēre, ursī press, urge, encroach on

uterus, -ī, *m.* belly

utrimque *adv.* on both sides

V

vādō, -ere proceed, go

valeō, -ēre, valuī be strong, fare well

validus, -a, -um powerful, strong

vallēs, -is, *f.* valley, vale

vānus, -a, -um false, groundless, unreliable, foolish

vehō, -ere, vexī, vectus carry, convey, transport

vellō, -ere, vellī *or* **vulsī, vulsus** pull out, pull up, extract, tear out, pull apart, tear down

vēlox, vēlōcis swift, rapid, speedy

vēnātor, vēnātōris, *m.* hunter

vēnātrix, vēnātrīcis, *f.* female hunter

ventōsus, -a, -um windy; lacking substance; changeable; vain

Venulus, -ī, *m.* Venulus, comrade of Turnus

Venus, Veneris, *f.* Venus, goddess of love; love

veprēs, -ium, *m. pl.* thornbush, brambles

verberō (1) beat, strike, batter

verbum, -ī, *n.* word, utterance

vērō *adv.* truly

verrō, -ere sweep, pass over (a surface)

versō (1) turn, turn over, keep turning over, revolve, ponder

vertex, verticis, *m.* top of the head, crown

vērum *adv.* but

victrix, victrīcis, *f.* conqueror, victorious one

vinc(u)lum, -ī, *n.* chain, bond, fetter

violō (1) violate, defile

virgātus, -a, -um striped

virgineus, -a, -um of a maiden, maidenly, virginal

virginitās, virginitātis, *f.* virginity

viridis, -e green

viscus, visceris, *n.* innards, internal organs

volātilis, -e able to fly, flying

Volcānus, -ī, *m.* Vulcan, god of fire

volitō (1) flit about, fly, move rapidly about, flutter

volō (1) fly, move swiftly

Volscī, -ōrum, *m. pl.* Volscians, a people of Latium

volūmen, volūminis, *n.* roll, coil, twist

vomō, -ere, vomuī, vomitus discharge, spew forth, vomit, pour forth, emit

vōtum, -ī, *n.* vow, promise, prayer, offering

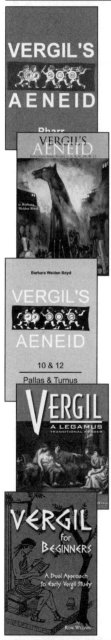

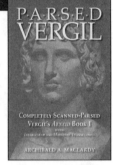
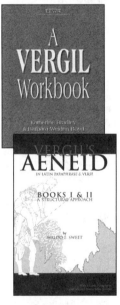

VERGIL MATERIALS TO ENRICH COMPREHENSION

VERGIL'S *AENEID:* Hero, War, Humanity
G. B. Cobbold

A novelized English version of the entire *Aeneid*, with engaging and helpful reader aids.

xviii + 366 pp. (2005) Paperback, ISBN 978-0-86516-596-0

POET & ARTIST: Imaging the *Aeneid*
Henry V. Bender and David Califf

Book/CD combination that juxtaposes images with the AP* text of Vergil and thought-provoking questions. Encourages students to examine the text more closely and reflect critically upon it.

xvi + 88 pp. (2004) Paperback + CD-ROM, ISBN 978-0-86516-585-4

THE ART OF THE AENEID, 2nd edition
William S. Anderson

"A useful start on Rome's finest poem,"according to William S. Anderson. Background on Vergil and the genre of epic, followed by analysis of each of the twelve books in turn.

vi + 138 pp. (2005, 2nd ed., 1989 reprint of 1969 ed.)
Paperback, ISBN 978-0-86516-598-4

WHY VERGIL? A Collection of Interpretations
Stephanie Quinn, ed.

43 selections by 38 authors, with Quinn's powerful, extensive Introduction and Conclusion.

xxi + 451 pp. (2000)
Paperback, ISBN 978-0-86516-418-5
Hardbound, ISBN 978-0-86516-435-2

THE LABORS OF AENEAS:
What A Pain It Was to Found the Roman Race
Rose Williams

A delightful retelling of Vergil's entire *Aeneid* that is faithful to the story's facts, but told in a witty, droll fashion.

vi + 108 pp. (2003) Paperback, ISBN 978-0-86516-556-4

BOLCHAZY-CARDUCCI PUBLISHERS, INC.
WWW.BOLCHAZY.COM

VERGIL DRAMATICALLY READ AND PERFORMED

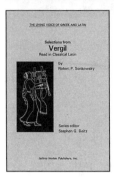

As Vergil's poetry, like most literature of its day, was meant to be read aloud, appreciation of it can be vastly enhanced by the use of oral materials.

VERGIL: SELECTIONS
Robert P. Sonkowsky

Classroom Edition, Language Lab

This set of two cassette tapes features two hours of selections from the *Aeneid* and some forty-five minutes of the *Eclogues* and the *Georgics* dramatically read in Latin by Robert Sonkowsky, Professor of Classics at the University of Minnesota and professional actor.

The readings incorporate the **Restored Classical pronunciation of Latin** formed upon the scholarly conclusions of historical linguists.

Selections:

Cassette 1 Side 1 (44 mins.)
Aeneid I, 1–156, 223–296, 223–296

Cassette 1 Side 2 (44 mins.)
Aeneid II, 40–56, 199–267, 469–558, 721–794, IV, 65–195, 296–415

Cassette 2 Side 1 (45 mins.)
Aeneid VI, 264–294, 417–476, 679–751, 54–901, VIII, 205–267, IX, 314–350, XI, 336–444, XII, 887–952

Cassette 2 Side 2 (46 mins.)
Eclogues I, II, & IV, *Georgics* IV, 315–566

(1985) Two Cassette Tapes, Order Number: 23685

VERGIL'S DIDO & MIMUS MAGICUS
Jan Novak, Composer; Rafael Kubelik, Conductor
Performed by the Symphony Orchestra of the Bayerischer Rundfunk

Adaptions of *Aeneid* IV and *Eclogue* VII, in lively recited and beautifully sung Latin.

Limited Edition CD (1997), 40 page libretto in Latin, English, and German
ISBN 978-0-86516-346-1

ROME'S GOLDEN POETS
St. Louis Chamber Chorus

Selections from Catullus, Vergil, and Horace.

Limited Edition CD, ISBN 978-0-86516-474-1

BOLCHAZY-CARDUCCI PUBLISHERS, INC.
WWW.BOLCHAZY.COM